Lia Barelli

The monumental complex of Santi Quattro Coronati in Rome

Translation by Christopher McDowall

viella

First edition: December 2009
ISBN 978-88-8334-426-8

Photographs by Gianfranco Zecca, unless otherwise indicated
Graphic diagrams by the author, revised by Lucia D. Simeone
Layout: Daniele Cesarini/Ervin

This book has been published also thanks to the contributions of

- Arte Colosseo, Via di S. Giovanni, Roma
- Arch. Cesare Esposito
- Federagit - Confesercenti - Guide Turistiche di Roma
- Virginio Franciosi, pittura e ristrutturazioni interni ed esterni
- Peronti - Servizio autorizzato Lancia e Multimarche, Via dei Santi Quattro, Roma
- SO.C.R.ED. srl - Società Costruzioni Restauri Edili, Roma
- Luigi Sparaco
- Studio di architettura Tamburini, Roma
- Famiglia Trombadori, in memory of Antonello and Fulvia Trombadori
- Itala and Vinicio Vici
- Hotel Capo d'Africa, Roma
- Volpetti, Roma

viella
Libreria editrice
via delle Alpi, 32
I-00198-ROMA
tel. 06 84 17 758
fax 06 85 35 39 60
www.viella.it

Contents

General plan of the complex

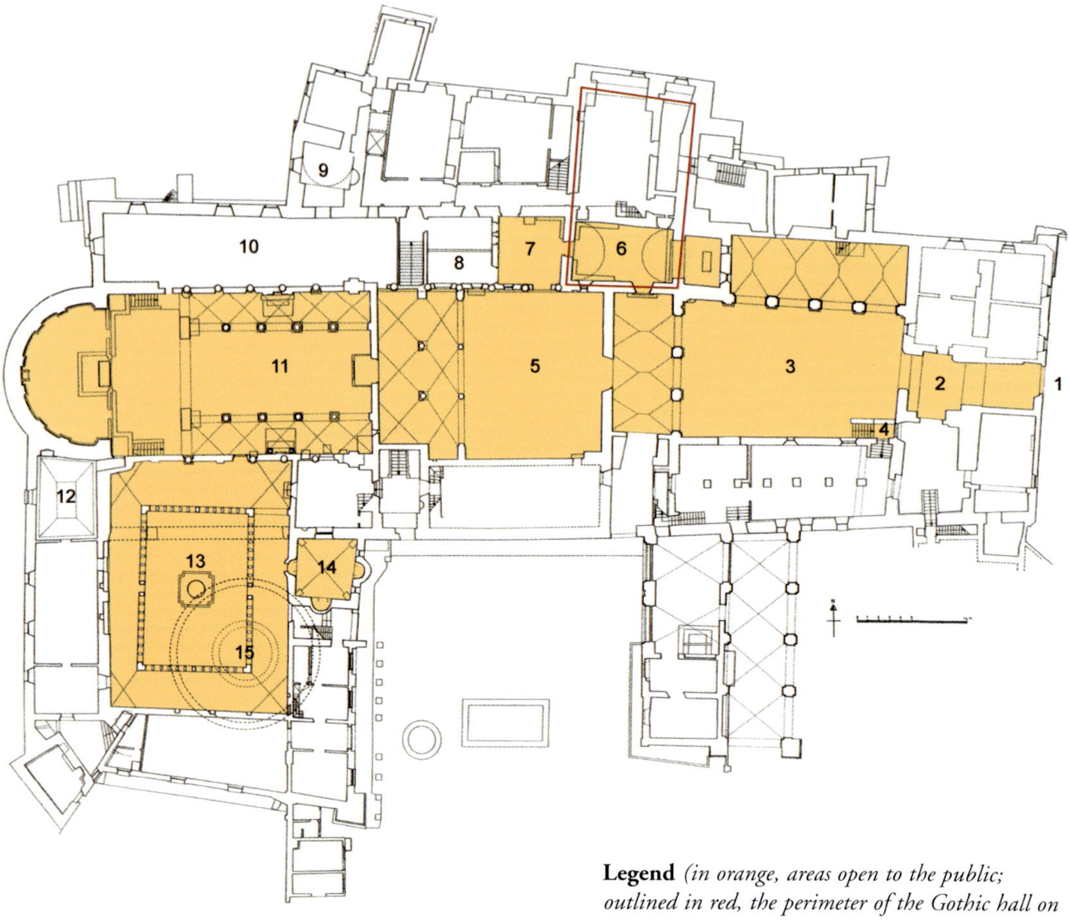

Legend *(in orange, areas open to the public; outlined in red, the perimeter of the Gothic hall on the first floor)*

1. Entrance to the complex
2. Tower of Leo IV
3. First courtyard
4. Entrance to the monastery of the Little Sisters of the Lamb
5. Second courtyard
6. Chapel of St Sylvester
7. Entrance hall to the Monastery of the Augustinian Nuns and *Calendar* room
8. Parlour of the Augustinian Nuns
9. Chapel of St Nicholas
10. Refectory of the Augustinian Nuns
11. Basilica
12. Sacristy
13. Cosmati cloister
14. Chapel of St Barbara
15. Site of baptistry (*dotted lines*)

1. Introduction

The sensations experienced by visitors as they approach the Santi Quattro Coronati complex vary according to the route they have chosen. For those arriving from Piazza San Giovanni along the initial flat and tranquil stretch of Via dei Ss. Quattro, its appearance in the distance at the back of a small square appears somewhat diminished, and it is only the tall brick tower rising above the façade that suggests the importance and antiquity of the structures. It is as we gradually get closer and the view becomes wider that we perceive some imposing towered structures to the right in the background.

For those arriving, instead, from the valley of the Colosseum along one of the many roads that lead from there to San Giovanni, the high walls of the complex

Fig. 1. *The entrance façade comprising the building that replaced the 9th-century portico, dominated by the tower of Leo IV (photo: L. Barelli).*

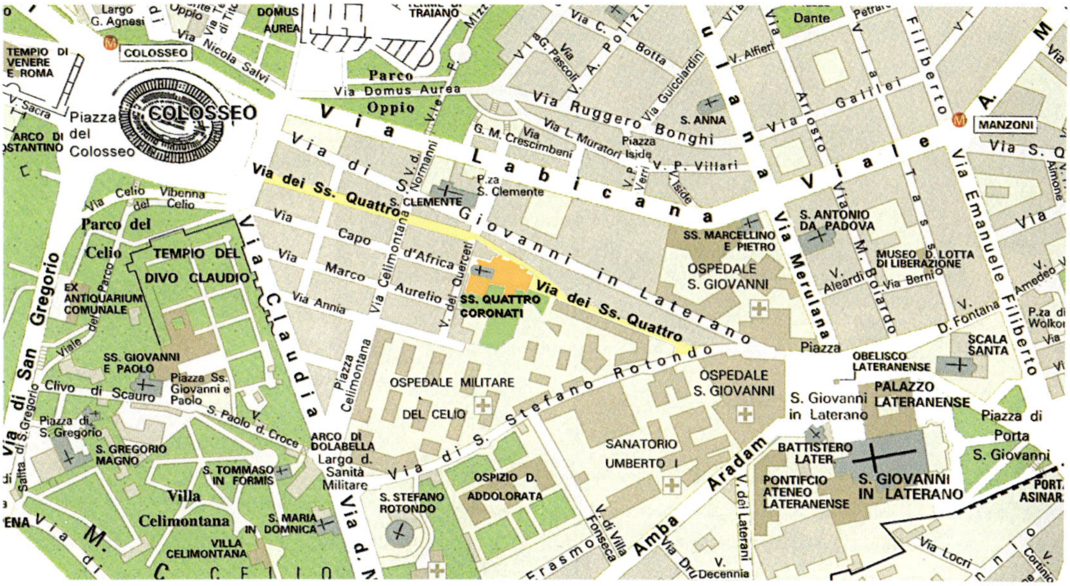

Fig. 2. *Map of existing routes that run from the Ss. Quattro complex towards San Giovanni in Laterano and the valley of the Colosseum.*

Fig. 3. *View of the complex from the west in a photograph of 1879 before the building development of the surrounding area (from Muñoz,* Il restauro, *tab. II).*

appear unexpectedly among the houses, with the apse rising almost like a defensive tower. This impression of a massive stronghold increases as one gets closer and admires the mighty 13th-century structures flanking both sides of the apse: to the right, a tall building terminating with a corner tower; to the left, along the steep rise leading to the small square at the entrance, formidable fortifications.

With regard to this, we must bear in mind that before the urban development of the area that surrounds it, the majority of which took place from 1870 onwards, from a distance the complex resembled a grand isolated fortress and in 1881 the renowned historian from Rome, Pasquale Adinolfi, referred to it with these words: "This was a building not to be underestimated along with Castel St Angelo and the other more fortified Roman structures".

If, despite the transformations of the surrounding area, this image of a closed and towered structure still undoubtedly has a strong impact on the visitor, the latter, as we shall see, represents only one of the many aspects of historical and artistic interest of what is one of the most complex and multilayered monuments in Rome, and precisely for this reason, also one of the most fascinating.

In these few pages, to make it easier for the visitor, I have had to (and have done so with much pleasure) condense the results of my studies on the complex of Santi Quattro Coronati, which started almost twenty years ago and are still destined, I hope, to explore further avenues of research. Given the importance of the monument and the dense network of connections that link it to the ancient and modern history of the city, I have come into contact with numerous experts and institutions, whose assistance has been substantial and, in some cases, invaluable. My heartfelt thanks go to all of them. In the many years I have dedicated to this research, however, the support I received from dear Mother Rita Mancini, prioress of the Augustinian monastery of Ss. Quattro, has more than any other been indispensable; she wished for this new and updated guide, but was sadly unable to see it completed.

2. The patron saints

One of the first questions that the visitor poses concerns the identity of the Four Crowned Saints. This is one of the most intricate questions in hagiography, about which rivers of ink have already been consumed and that, in this guide it is only possible to touch upon. It is almost certain that their name refers to the crown of martyrdom. Furthermore, this name has been applied to two groups of martyrs, one foreign and one Roman, whose life stories, no doubt enriched by fanciful details, have been passed down to us through a *passio* (a term indicating ancient hagiographical writings in which history and legend become interwoven) dating from around the 6th century onwards. These stories also represent the source of the iconography of many works of art that, as we shall see, are present within the complex, which is why it is worth recording them in detail.

The first group of martyrs consists surprisingly of five, not four saints: Claudius, Castorius, Simpronianus, Nicostratus and Simplicitus, all stonemasons who, along with many others, worked for the emperor Diocletian in the quarries of Pannonia (today territories of former Yugoslavia). The first four were particular-

Fig. 4. *Giovanni da San Giovanni, frescoes in the apse:* Nicetius drops the five stonemasons enclosed in lead boxes into the river.

Fig. 5. *Giovanni da San Giovanni, frescoes in the apse:* St Sebastian and Pope Melchiades bury the bodies of the four Roman soldiers on Via Labicana.

ly admired by the emperor for their skills, who was unaware, however, that this was a divine gift deriving from their Christian faith that they professed in secret. They converted Simplicitus, had him baptized by Bishop Cyril, at that time a prisoner in Pannonia, and all together they continued to work in a miraculous way arousing envy on all sides. When Diocletian asked them to carve a statue of the god Asclepius, the five, who had already made a statue of the Sun-God for him, refused. It was easy at that moment for their envious colleagues to accuse them of sacrilege and magic. The tribune Lampadius was given the task of conducting the investigation and, to this end, ordered the stonemasons to venerate the statue of the Sun-God that they themselves had carved, but in vain. On Diocletian's orders, he decreed their death by *scorpiones* - to be beaten to death with gnarled and thorny sticks - but was unable to witness the martyrdom, as he died unexpectedly "seized by an evil spirit". Diocletian, offended by the death of Lampadius and by his wife's distress, ordered Nicetius, the tribune's assistant, to throw the five stonemasons into the river enclosed in five lead boxes. The martyrdom took place on 8 November and then Cyril, by now weary, passed away. After forty-two days, the Christian Nicodemus found the boxes with the bodies and took them to his home. The story of the *passio* ends at this point, without specifying what happened to the remains of the five stonemasons and how their cult arrived in Rome.

The second group of martyrs consists of four anonymous Roman soldiers holding the rank of *cornicularii* in Diocletian's employ. Their story, told in the *passio* following that of the stonemasons, has some elements in common with the latter. Because the four of them refused to offer sacrifice to the god Asclepius in the temple of the Baths of Trajan, the emperor condemned them to death by *plumbatae* - to be beaten with whips armed with lead balls at the end of each cord. After the martyrdom, their corpses were offered as food for dogs that, however, refused to devour them. The bodies, which remained unburied for five days, were retrieved at night by St Sebastian together with Pope Melchiades and interred in a cemetery on Via Labicana. As the martyrdom took place two years earlier, but on the same day as that of the five stonemasons, and their names were unknown, Melchiades commanded that their feast should be "celebrated under the names of Claudius, Nicostratus, Simpronianus and Castorius".

The confusion as to the identity of the Crowned Martyrs was further complicated by the fact that, at a later date, the identity of the four soldiers was supposedly miraculously revealed to a holy man: they were called Severus, Severianus, Carpophorus and Victorinus, names in reality that coincide with those of four

Fig. 6. *The apse with the frescoes of Giovanni da San Giovanni narrating the stories of the four Roman soldiers (above) and of the five Pannonian stonemasons (below).*

Fig. 7. *Giovanni Baglione, detail of the altarpiece of St Sebastian, depicting* San Sebastian cared for by Lucina and Irene *(1632).*

martyrs venerated since the 4th century at the catacombs of Albano, with the exception of the first of these latter named Secundus.

The *Passio* of St Sebastian, where the fanciful nature of the story is even greater, also includes the stories of certain martyrs, which contribute to confusing the complex issue. Here we have two sets of brothers, Nicostratus and Castorius, and Claudius and Victorinus as well as Claudius' son Simpronianus, all of Roman nationality, who were weighted down and thrown into the sea. The similarity to the martyrdom of the stonemasons is evident, even though this form of death was generally attributed to those martyrs whose bodies were not preserved, a fact that made this easy to justify. In this case, the names of four of the stonemasons and one of the Albano martyrs recur!

The authenticity of these stories has been much discussed, but without reaching any conclusion. From the historical standpoint, the few certain facts seem those recorded in the *Depositio Martyrum* (the first calendar of martyrs of the Church of Rome dating to the early 4th century AD), where four martyrs are recorded, only three of which would then be identified in the Pannonian group: Clement, Simpronianus, Claudius and Nicostratus, venerated "in comitatum" (an expression that has been interpreted both as a place name and attributed to an imperial estate on Via Labicana known as *ad duas* lauros [near the two laurels], and as meaning "together"). Their feast (that corresponds to the day of the martyrdom) was celebrated on 7 November, though it must be noted that this varied between the 7th and 9th in the ancient sources, and that only in the modern age was it fixed by mutual consent on the 8th day of the month. The same source on the 8 August also cites the Albano martyrs Secundus, Carpophorus, Victorinus and Severianus.

The *Itineraries*, guides compiled between the 7th and 8th century for the pilgrims arriving in Rome and generally fairly reliable as regards topographical information, then attest to the burial of the four martyrs in the cemetery of Sts Peter and Marcellinus on Via Labicana, where a cubiculum is inscribed with the name Clement, probably the first martyr cited in the *Depositio.*

Uniting the data available, the simplest interpretation of the identity of the Crowned Martyrs is that they were Roman, perhaps soldiers, buried in Via Labicana, whose feast day was present in the local calendars, but about whom so little was known that, with the passing of time, they ended up being referred to as a group.

How then do we explain the aggregation of the stonemasons, whose martyrdom actually took place at an earlier date, to these? It is possible that the refugees fleeing Pannonia as a result of the pressure placed on them by the barbarian populations starting from the late 5th-early 6th century, brought the cult of their own martyrs to Rome, among them the stonemasons that either because they bore in part the same names or because their relics were transferred to the cemetery of Via Labicana, finished up overlapping with the Roman group. The question, however, remains open.

The confusion was also apparent in the Early Middle Ages and it is likely that Pope Leo IV (847-855) thought he would resolve the question once and for all. It appears, in fact, possible to deduce from the words of the *Liber Pontificalis* (the text that chronicles the ancient papal biographies) that this pope, who reconstructed, as we shall see, the entire architectonic complex of Santi Quattro Coronati in a grandiose style, organized a search for the relics of the four soldiers, the five stonemasons and the martyrs of Albano and had them all placed together in the crypt of the basilica. In this way, he ensured that the relics of the eponymous martyrs would be venerated, whoever they were.

3. History of the complex

3.1. The pre-existing structures

The complex stands on a spur of the much larger Caelian Hill, perhaps what was called *Coeliolus* (Little Caelian) in antiquity that, as was easily noticeable before the intensive urban development of the area, joined up with the Lateran plateau to the south-east, while precipitously overlooking the valley that separates it from the Oppian Hill to the north-west. In ancient times this spur lay within the Republican walls and, in the 7th century BC, it became part of the Second of the Fourteen Regions into which Augustus divided up the city. A stretch of Via *Tusculana* (more or less today's Via dei Ss. Quattro) ran along its northern slopes and presumably crossed the walls at the so-called *Querquetulana* gate. It was therefore an area soon to be urbanized, in which uninterrupted building activity was to follow. As a result, like many of the historic buildings of the city, also the complex of Ss. Quattro Coronati stands on stratified archaeological remains of up to several metres in depth. Some of these can be seen in the underground areas (not open to the public) and many others have been recorded during excavations or from random discoveries, which took place in different epochs.

Despite the wealth of data available, however, faithfully reconstructing the history of the buildings that preceded those visible today is no easy task. If the identification of the area with the *Coeliolus* is correct, a sacellum dedicated to the

Fig. 8. *Map of the area of Ss. Quattro during the imperial age.*
Legend below:
a. Hypothetical reconstruction of road network.
b. Evident or known Roman structures.
c. Area occupied by the Ss. Quattro Coronati complex.

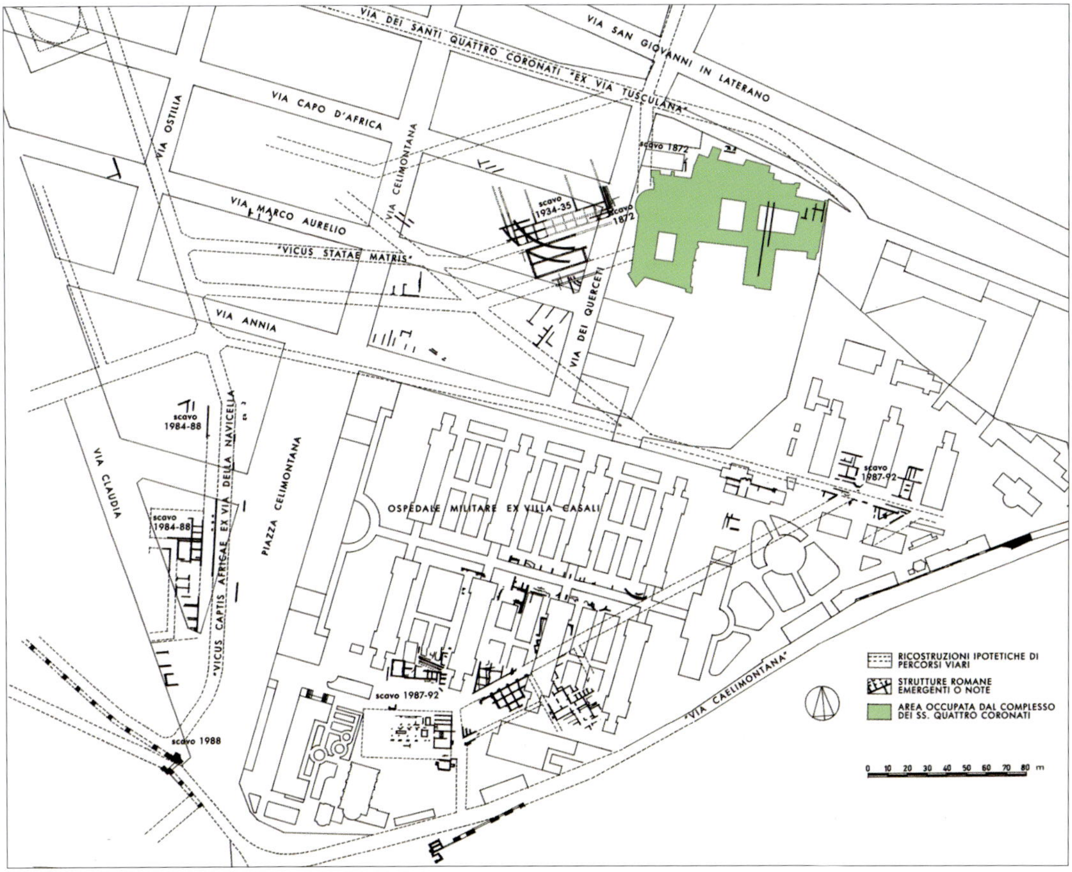

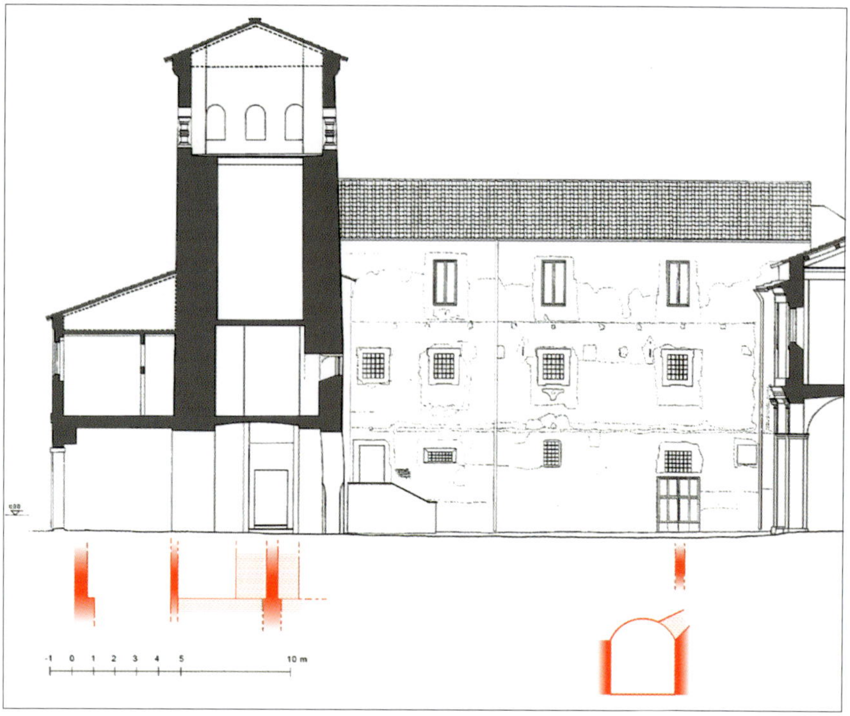

Fig. 9. *Elevation diagram of the first courtyard, with the currently known ancient Roman structures in red.*

cult of Diana, goddess of hunting and woods stood here during the Republican Age, which suggests that the area was originally wooded.

During the Imperial Age, in adherence with the process of urbanization over the entire Caelian Hill, simple dwellings and utilitarian structures thronged the lower slopes of the spur, while the summit was reserved for the construction of luxury residences. Although the orographic configuration is difficult to perceive, mainly due to the progressive elevation of the terrain at the bottom of the valley, the site where the complex stands boasts a fine panoramic view that most certainly favoured its use for prestigious buildings. In fact, the emperor Nero chose a

Fig. 10. *Existing Roman structures below the entrance façade block.*

Fig. 11. *The cryptoporticus (c. 2nd cent. AD) situated below the first courtyard.*

similar site on the other side of the valley to erect the *Domus Aurea*, his immense and sumptuous residence constructed after the fire in 64 BC. On the other hand, already prior to this, Cicero had recorded that the sacellum dedicated to Diana on the *Coeliolus* was replaced by the house of Lucius Calpurnius Pisus Cesoninus, the influential politician, father of Calpurnia, the wife of Julius Caesar.

In support of the above, below the first courtyard of the complex we find a cryptoporticus dating to the 1st or 2nd century AD and, above it, remains of rooms that had been heated perhaps from the 4th century, which testify to the sequence of building structures on the site designed for well-to-do families. Precisely during the 4th century the *Regionary Catalogues* (ancient inventories of buildings, divided into quarters of the city, of a pre-Constantine era) reveal the presence of as many as 127 *domus* on the Caelian Hill. Among them were villas of senatorial or even imperial ownership and it is likely that one of these occupied our site. Confirmation of this lies in the imposing structures, dating to this century, which trace out a vast apsidal hall, identified with the reception area of a luxurious *domus* of noble status. In order to build the hall, 42 m in length and 15 m wide, many of the pre-existing structures were destroyed and a public road was put out of use. This practice is not unlike what happened in the 4th century when large residential complexes extending over vast areas were constructed in Rome, which, in their turn, modified the road network.

The construction of the hall that, as we shall see, was used as a place of Christian worship conditioned all the later transformations of the complex, determining the layout and orientation of the new structures up until the modern age.

3.2. The first centuries of life of the Christian settlement (5th - 9th c.)

Before the year 595, when a *Fortunatus presbyter tituli sanctorum quattuor Coronatorum* participated in the synod held by Pope Gregory the Great, a *titulus*

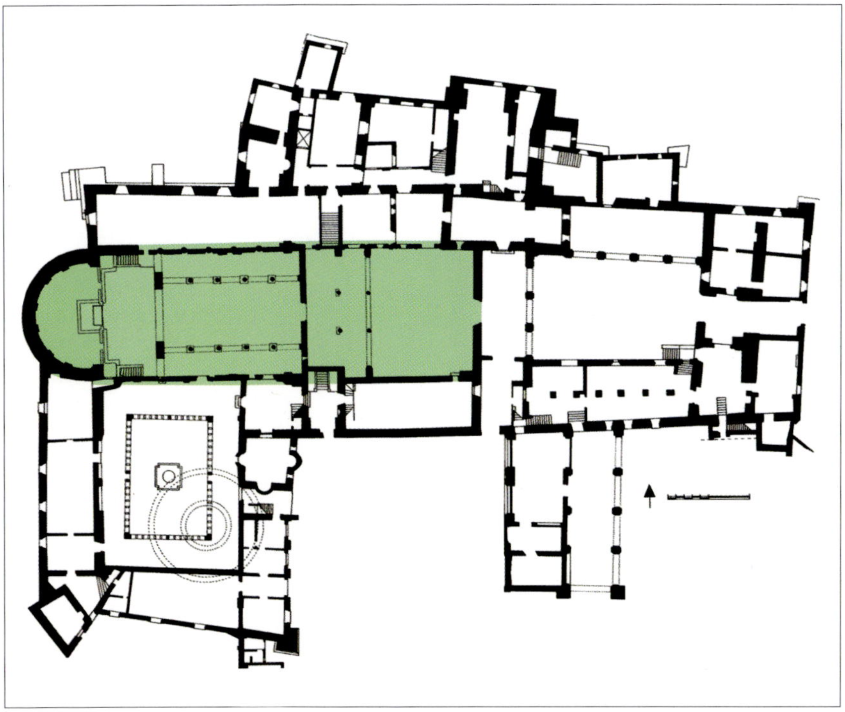

Fig. 12. *Extent of the 4th-century hall (in green) with respect to the existing plan of the complex.*

was established within the structures of the *domus*, namely an institution in use in Rome comparable to today's parish. When exactly this occurred and how long ago the *titulus* was dedicated to the Four Crowned Martyrs, is unknown, but it is however possible to make a number of hypotheses.

According to some, the *titulus* supposedly already existed in the first half of the 5th century, a period during which a citation in the *Geronimian Martyrology* (a universal calendar of the Church) can be dated, where in the month of November the feast dedicated to the martyrs celebrated "*Romae ad Celio monte*" (in Rome on the Caelian Hill) is mentioned. The lack of citations during the period between these two sources could be explained by the identification of the *titulus* dedicated to the Four Crowned Martyrs with the more ancient *titulus Aemilianae*, of which the first mention relates to the synod of 499. Also in other cases, it has been ascertained that a *titulus* originally designated by the name of its founder, in this a case a noblewoman named Emiliana, later adopted the name of the martyrs venerated within it.

Moreover, the recent excavations in the cloister (2002-2004), which brought to light a large circular baptistry dating to the mid-5th century, would seem to point to this conclusion. Its architectural importance (the size of the font is second only in Rome to that of the Lateran baptistry) indicates that the *titulus* must not only have existed before 595, but also played a significant role in the city.

Despite this, also 7th and 8th-century sources on the history of the complex are scarce, although not devoid of interest: the *Liber Pontificalis*, in fact, states that Pope Honorius I "fecit ecclesiam beatorum martyrum Quattuor Coronatorum quem et dedicavit, et donum obtulit". There are no identifiable archaeological traces of this work, apart perhaps from a few marble fragments of liturgical fittings. It is therefore supposed that his intervention, previously considered to have been a full-scale reconstruction, consisted in readjusting the already existing structures (presumably those of the hall of the *domus*), as the same pope had done in other cases.

Again the *Liber Pontificalis* records that Hadrian I (772-795) rebuilt the roofs of the *titulus* replacing the beams: an exacting work made necessary by its poor state of repair, which seems justified only by the already supposed ancient nature of the structures that Honorius I simply reutilized.

Fig. 13. *The archaeological excavation of the central cloister area (2002-2004, sponsors: Antigua Foundation and Robert Wilson). In the top left corner, the circular perimeter of the baptismal font.*

Fig. 14. Detail of the interior of the baptismal font (photo: R. Pugliese).

3.3. The reconstruction by Leo IV (847-855)

It is only with the 9th century that the information provided by documents can be directly related to the visible structures, corresponding moreover to one of the most important phases of the entire complex. It is in this century, in fact, that we see the establishment in Rome of the so-called Carolingian Renaissance, and precisely in the year 847, that the cardinal priest of Ss. Quattro Coronati became pope under the name of Leo IV. Up until his death he maintained an intimate link with his *titulus*, where he was actively involved in helping the poor and the pilgrims. Among his first concerns was therefore that of reconstructing the complex – that despite the work of Hadrian I was by then in a dilapidated state - in a truly magnificent way for the age.

On completion of the work done by Leo IV, arriving from the Cathedral of San Giovanni, we would first encounter a portico formed by arches on columns alternating with pillars (incorporated in the present façade) dominated by the massive tower, still in existence today. Three doors led one into a monumental quadriporticus of a rectangular plan (more or less corresponding to the existing first courtyard), whose colonnaded wings were separated from one another by four great arches positioned in the corners. The tower rose upwards from the centre of the east wing, its base entirely pierced by arches to facilitate entry below it. Another three doors led from the west wing into the basilica. The latter, a structure of considerable dimensions (55 m in length and 30 m wide), had three aisles with arcades surmounted by an architrave on either side of the nave and an apse with an underlying semi-annular crypt. In the latter, the pope transferred an impressionable quantity of relics among them, it is said, those of the eponymous martyrs. The side aisles were without windows, whereas the central nave was illuminated from all sides: three windows in both the façade and the apse, others corresponding to the intercolumniation ran above the arcades. Lastly, several chapels were symmetrically positioned at right angles to the longitudinal walls.

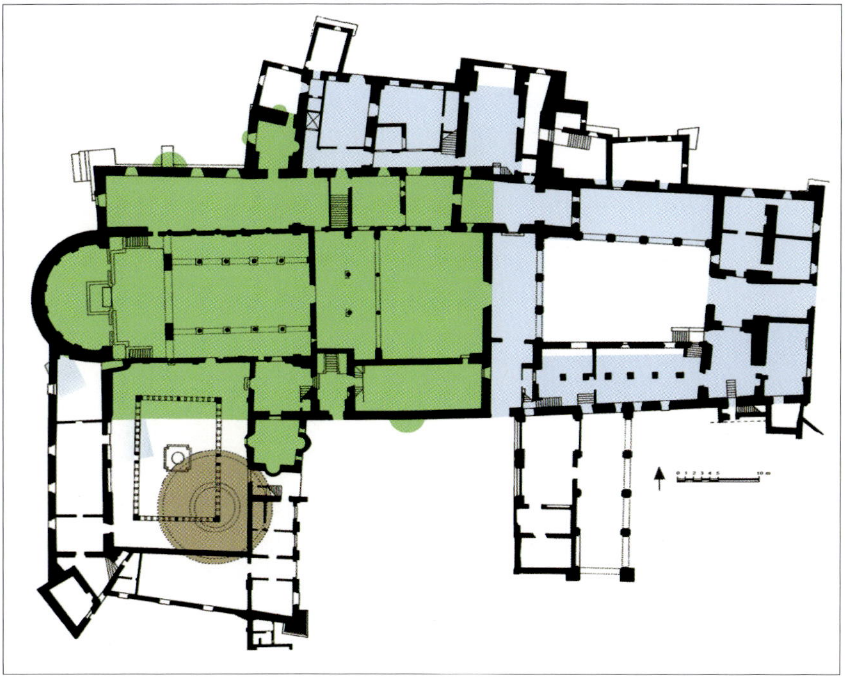

Fig. 15. Verified extent of the complex in the 9th century with respect to the existing plan: in green, the basilica and oratories; in blue, the annexes; in beige, the pre-existing baptistry.

The walls of the hall of the *domus* were lowered and used as a foundation base for the central nave, in such a way that the latter retraced the pre-existing form: in particular, we can see from the outside that the substructure of the apse still comprises that of Late Antiquity. And it is precisely this reuse of the most ancient walls, also evident at other points in the Leonine structure, which explains the asymmetry and irregularities present in the plan, which were, however, skilfully concealed in reality.

A building of trapezoidal plan then backed onto the right side of the complex, probably used as a residence for the clergy. On the left side of the basilica, instead, traces identified during the archaeological excavations of a door followed by some steps, which coincided with that of the baptistry, indicate that the latter continued to be in use. Furthermore, right next to the baptistry, excavations brought to light traces of a room dating to the 9th century, perhaps the sacristy, whose position lies very close by even today. This latter room had an orientation different from that of the walls of the basilica and therefore from the Late Antiquity structures, but similar to an *insula* from the 1st-2nd century AD situated at the west of the complex, which at the time of Leo IV was not only in use but was also raised in height. One of its corners was incorporated in the apse, traces of which can still be seen today.

Finally, it cannot be excluded that already from the time of Leo IV, a *cella* (a term that describes a monastic settlement) may have been in existence at the basilica, in evidence at least since 975, when Pope Benedict VII entrusted it with all its effects to Theodericus, archbishop of Trier.

As far as the technical aspects are concerned, it is evident that the foundations and Leonine substructures were constructed with large tufa blocks and the elevations with bricks, both materials salvaged from ancient buildings and laid without much regularity, much like the constructions of the period in Rome. The surfaces both inside and out, however, had a different aspect to their present one, in

Fig. 16. *Lower Church of San Clemente, portrait of Pope Leo IV (844-857). Restored by the Istituto Superiore per la Conservazione ed il Restauro (Ministry for Cultural Properties and Activities) in 2008 (photo: ISCR).*

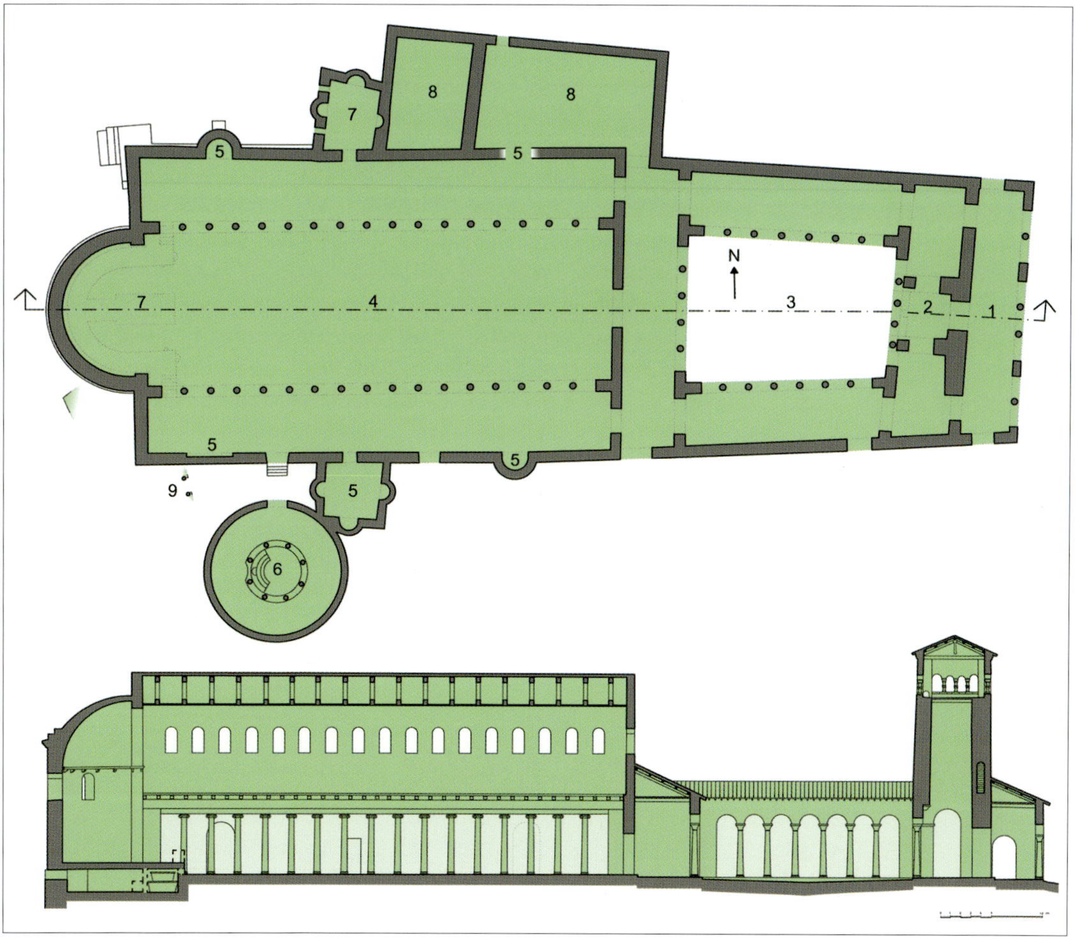

Fig. 17. *Hypothetical reconstruction of the plan and elevation diagram of complex at the time of Leo IV (847-855):*
1. Portico;
2. Base of tower;
3. Quadriporticus;
4. Basilica;
5. Oratories;
6. Baptistry;
7. Crypt;
8. Residence;
9. Sacristy(?).

that these materials often remained visible: they were plastered and frescoed and the overall result was vivid and multicoloured. Added to this, pieces of sculpture mainly deriving from Roman buildings, were inserted everywhere to embellish the architectonic elements, such as the doorframes and cornices that capped the walls. Lastly, splendid liturgical fittings enriched the interior of the basilica.

In conclusion, the vast dimensions, the architectural quality, the richness of the decorative elements and the exceptional importance of the relics placed in the crypt testify that Leo IV made every effort to transform his *titulus* into a monument that stood out among all others of that era.

3.4. The Norman fire (1084) and the works of Pascal II (1099-1118)

In the 11th century the life of the complex was upset by a catastrophic event. In 1084, after the Norman prince Robert Guiscard had put the emperor Henry IV – who had entered Rome with his army - to flight in order to assist Gregory VII, the city was violently sacked and parts of it were set on fire. The fire engulfed the complex of Ss. Quattro Coronati and caused the nave and part of the apse to collapse.

Many years passed before Pope Pascal II (1099-1118) attempted an initial restoration aimed at maintaining not only the original dimensions, but also many of the figurative features of the Leonine church, such as the light-filled nave contrasting with the dark aisles, and the cornices with marble corbels capping the walls. A few variations, however, were introduced, among them the replacement of the architrave on the columns with arches and the insertion of a cruciform pilaster at the centre of the two arcades (similar to what the same pope had done in the Basilica of San Clemente).

The works that commenced from the apse were, however, interrupted, when the building had reached different stages of completion, and in particular, before starting the east sector of the left arcade. The reasons for this interruption were probably economic, but also of a practical nature: as a result of the fire that had hit the surrounding area, and of the consequent demise of its inhabitants, the parish had become useless without its congregation, as had their vast Leonine place of worship. Pascal II therefore decided, albeit reluctantly, to reduce the space for worship to that occupied by the existing basilica, in other words, only the west half of the former nave. A smaller nave with aisles on both sides was constructed within this space, in which the latter were surmounted by galleries and a transept, while the apse remained in its pre-existing form. The remaining part of the former nave, without its roof, became a second atrium, in which a new portico was created in front of the smaller church, while the two former side aisles, left and right respectively, were progressively incorporated into a monastery founded by Pascal II himself and a residence for the titular clergy. Pascal's church, enhanced with new fittings, was consecrated on 20 January 1116.

Fig. 18. *Plan of the north-west section of the complex indicating the structures of the basilica of Leo IV preserved after the fire of 1084 (in green), the parts reconstructed under Pascal II (1099-1118) in the first Romanic phase (in light blue), and those constructed by the same pope in the second Romanic phase (in dark blue).*

Fig. 19. *The pavement of the basilica of Pasquale II (1099-1118) as seen from above.*

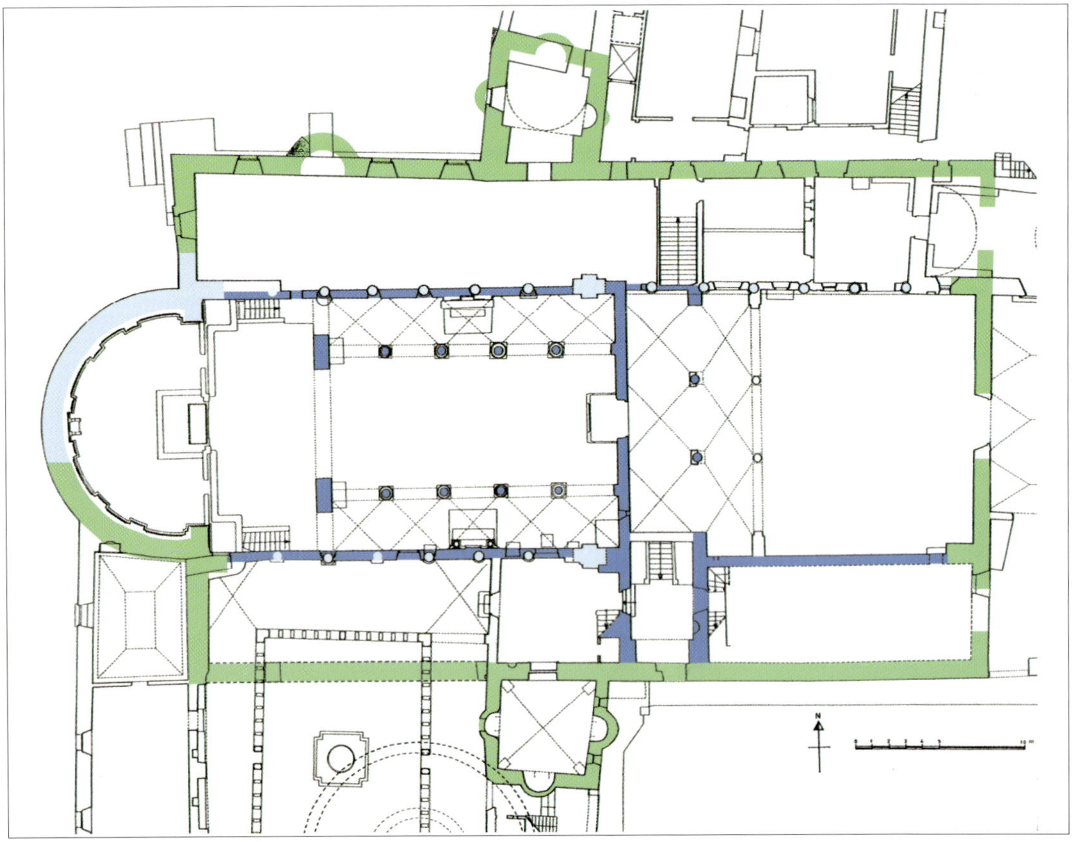

3.5. The Benedictine monastery (12th – 14th c.)

After 975, it is necessary to arrive at the pontificate of Pascal II for further sources on the presence of a monastery at Ss. Quattro. In 1116, he entrusted the recently restored basilica together with the nearby church of S. Maria in Monasterio Michaeli to a community of monks to whom he gave the task of maintaining the Divine Office in the basilica.

Nothing is known for certain about the first structures inhabited by the monks, but it seems that they may have immediately reused the former left aisle of the Leonine basilica. To it, they added a first cloister on a square plan, whose construction necessitated the demolition of the baptistry, damaged by the fire and by then also useless without the parish. In 1138, this monastic settlement had become one of the priories of the influential Benedictine abbey of Santa Croce di Sassovivo near Foligno in Umbria, and from then on it also fulfilled the function of a temporary residence for the abbots visiting the pope as well as hosting many visitors from Foligno connected to the abbey, with the result that it was sometimes referred to as *castrum folignatorum.* It had numerous properties in the city, among them many houses close to the complex and its moment of full splendour arrived at the same time as the mother house during the first half of the 13th century, when a splendid Cosmati cloister as well as a *palatium dormidorii,* the building containing the monastic cells, were constructed in both monasteries.

Fig. 20. *Head of Benedictine monk carved onto one of the cloister colonnettes (photo: L. Barelli).*

Subsequently, however, the rapid decay of the abbey likewise affected the Roman priory, as a list drawn up in 1315 of the sacred furnishings of the basilica belonging to the monks would seem to testify, presenting a picture of abject poverty. Even though the monks present at the time of the compilation of the so-called Catalogue of Turin (a list of the churches in Rome dating from 1313-1339) still numbered ten, the importance of the institution had declined considerably and, as a consequence, any development of its building structures was brought to a standstill.

3.6. The Cardinal's Palace (12th – 14th c.)

From around the second half of the 12th century until 1338, no new cardinals were elected to the *titulus* of Ss. Quattro. This fact, in spite of what it may seem, is not indicative of a decline in importance or of abandon. On the contrary, during the course of the 13th century the residence of the titular clergy, situated on the right flank of the complex, was transformed into a grand palace complete with towers and other fortification works. Probably the greater part of it was commissioned by Stefano Conti (d. 1254), Cardinal of S. Maria in Trastevere, nephew of Pope Innocent III, appointed *Vicarius Urbis* in 1245, after Innocent IV had taken refuge in France following the dispute with the emperor Frederick II. And it was at least since the preceding year that records testify to the presence in the complex of Stefano Conti, to whom the residence may have already been assigned for several years, quite possibly even by his uncle Innocent III, who in this way would place a building of great strategic importance in the hands of his own family. Apart from being close to the Lateran, the complex was situated in a commanding position (as well as having a splendid panorama of the city) that ensured control over Via *maior* below (the road that connected the papal palace with the Vatican), and once it had been turned into a fortress it would become a safe haven even for the pope himself.

After the death of Stefano Conti, the popes entrusted the palace to other powerful cardinals, such as the extremely wealthy Ottaviano degli Ubaldini, Benedet-

Fig. 21. *Verified extent of the complex at the end of the 13th century with respect to the existing plan: in green, the basilica; in blue, the Cardinal's palace; in yellow, the Benedictine monastery.*

to Caetani (the future Boniface VIII) and his nephew Francesco, and likewise Arnaldo de Via, nephew of John XXII. Also leading lay figures such as the French prince, Charles of Anjou, who stayed there for two months in 1265, or the senator Henry of Castile, who signed the peace treaty between the Guelphs and Ghibellines in 1267 in his rooms, were guests.

At the apex of its expansion, the palace was extended to the east and north sectors of the complex, where it incorporated a large part of the Leonine structures by then abandoned, and included numerous buildings overlooking the two courtyards, the first partially retracing the Leonine atrium, the second obtained from the eastern side of the former nave. It was a noble residence providing maximum comfort, but also protected by the fortification works. As well as the recep-

Fig. 22. *The Great Tower (first half of 13th cent.) photographed from the tower of Leo IV (photo: L. Barelli).*

Fig. 23. *Detail of a youthful male figure above the candelabra motif frescoed on the east wall of the south bay of the Gothic hall.*

tion areas and private rooms, it contained other premises for day-to-day activities: kitchen, bakery, wine cellar, stables and latrines. There would also have been dormitories for the cardinals' retinue and servants, who were most likely allocated a separate refectory and other kitchens. Large cisterns provided a plentiful supply of water. Lastly, it seems that it also contained an additional residence for an important member of the retinue, such as the doctor or chaplain, consisting of a small building attached to the northern side of the complex.

Among the palace buildings, the Great Tower, whose construction we owe to Stefano Conti, on the north side of the complex, is of particular note, both for its considerable size (it rises more than 26 m from the present level of Via dei Ss. Quattro) and because it contains the main reception areas, namely the chapel of St Sylvester and the so-called Gothic Hall. The latter was also connected to a splendid gallery in the Gothic style that overlooked the first courtyard, constructed at a slightly later date.

The importance of the palace at the time of Stefano Conti is also attested by the extensive pictorial cycle that adorns its walls. Given all its architectonic characteristics, as well as the content of the frescoes that represent the superiority of papal over imperial power, it would seem reasonable to suppose that the palace of Stefano Conti was a kind of response by the powerful *Vicarius Urbis* to the noble residences that the emperor Frederick II had erected during his reign.

The building development of the palace took place almost at the same time as that of the monastery, so that by the end of the 13th century the whole complex appeared renewed in a grandiose style, bristling with towers and affording magnificent views from its Gothic windows and loggias.

3.7. Decay and abandon (15th – 16th c.)

In the 14th century, the transfer of the papal seat to Avignon led to a loss of interest in the palace that, combined with the effects produced by the decline of the abbey at Sassovivo, resulted in the entire complex being reduced to a state of abandon. Despite an ongoing dispute in 1340 between the monks and the titular cardinal Guillaume Court (1338-1350) regarding the possession of certain effects linked to the *titulus,* and the fact that the pope had specifically entrusted the use of the palace to Guillaume, it would seem that in practice it was no longer inhabited. The consequent lack of maintenance over the next few decades as well as the antiquity of many of the structures and, perhaps, the effects of the earthquake that hit Rome in 1348, made serious works of restoration necessary. Following the return of the papacy to Rome with Martin V (1417-1431), between 1423 and 1431 the cardinal, Alfonso Carrillo, provided large sums of money for these works, as the inscription above the arch of the passage leading into the first courtyard testifies. His intervention became part of the much more extensive restoration programme developed by Martin V, who was trying to resolve the widespread decay of religious buildings in Rome.

Following the works of Carrillo, the palace was again able to host a banquet for a figure of importance like Sigmund of Hungary in 1433. By then, however, although Callistus III Borgia (1455-1458), former titular cardinal, still took an interest at least in its maintenance, the decision to abandon the Lateran seat on the part of the popes and establish themselves permanently at the Vatican, vastly reduced the importance of the palace, to which the necessary attention was no longer devoted.

Also the monastic structures, even though they passed to the Camaldolensian Order through the intervention of the titular cardinal Lorenzo Pucci, the outcome did not improve its fortunes. The new arrivals, in fact, abandoned it immediately because of the unhealthiness of the air, maintaining only the office of Procurator of the Congregation on the site.

Fig. 24. *The coat-of-arms and inscription of the Spanish cardinal Alfonso Carrillo (1423-1434) situated above the pointed entrance arch of the first courtyard. The text reads: HEC QUECUMQUE VIDES VETERI PROSTRATA RUINA,/ OBRUTA VERBENIS EDERIS DUMISQUE IACEBANT/ NON TULIT HISPANUS CARRILLO ALFONSUS HONORE/ CARDINEO FULGENS X SED OPUS LICET OCCUPAT INGENS/ SIC ANIMUS MAGNO REPARATQUE PALATIA SUMPTU/ DUM SEDET EXTINCTO MARTINUS SCISMATE QUINTUS (All that you see was once lying on the ground prostrated like an ancient ruin, covered with verbena, ivy and brambles. The Spaniard Alfonso Carrillo, resplendent with the honour pertaining to a cardinal, was unable to endure it, and his determination led him to undertake the work of restoration despite the enormity of the task, and he had the buildings restored at great expense, while Martin V, having settled the schism, occupied the Throne of St Peter).*

3.8. The conservatory for orphaned girls and the monastery of the Augustinian Nuns (1562 – 21st c.)

In the mid-16th century the entire complex consequently fell yet again into serious disrepair. This negative state, however, due this time to years of neglect, was once again the origin of an important new chapter in its history.

In 1536, inspired by Ignatius Loyola, the Archconfraternity of S. Maria della Visitazione degli Orfani came into being, with the purpose of assisting the children of the city without parents: the boys were accommodated in the houses adjoining the church of S. Maria in Aquiro, where they stayed until they reached the age they could start an apprenticeship with a craftsman or artist; the girls lived in a house near Piazza di Pietra, where they were educated for marriage or monastic life. In 1548, a group of these orphans decided to found a monastery within the house to assist their younger companions and adopted the Augustinian Rule.

In 1560, due to the increasing number of young girls, but also to the limited privacy of their lodgings situated in the noisy Roman street, the Archconfraternity asked Pius IV for more appropriate accommodation. What could be better than the spacious religious complex, by then isolated among vineyards and orchards, which would not attract the interest of others, precisely because of its peripheral position, as well as its state of disrepair? The pope assigned it to the Archconfraternity in 1562 with the consent of the titular cardinal King Henry of Portugal (1547-1580), but the necessary and demanding works of restoration meant that the orphans were unable to move there until 12 March 1564, two years later.

In the meantime, at least since 1570, a new institution had been established in the complex: the University of Marble Workers, a Roman guild whose statute dates back to 1406, although it most certainly had more ancient origins. The Santi Quattro Coronati were its patron saints and, in 1577, it acquired the chapel of St Sylvester providing for its upkeep from then on.

Fig. 25. *Extent of the complex at the end of the 17th century with respect to the existing plan: in green, the basilica and chapel of St Sylvester; in yellow, the monastery and conservatory for orphaned girls.*

Fig. 26. *The nuns' habit and that of the orphans in two engravings by Arnold van Westerhout (1651-1725) (from F. Bonanni,* Catalogo degli ordini religiosi della Chiesa militante..., *Rome 1742, vol. II, tab. 7; vol. III, tab. 56).*

In the monastery, or rather in the conservatory of orphaned girls, as it was then called, the daily routine of the nuns and girls was divided between hours of study, prayer and work, but also included periods of rest and recreation. Apart from on rare occasions, however, such as the procession of 8 November, the day of the martyrdom of the Santi Quattro, when new arrivals were accompanied to the monastery, the girls lived a chaste and cloistered life along with the nuns.

Such a rigid form of existence led to certain adjustments to the building structures, but because of the economic difficulties of the institution and despite the help from the protector cardinals of the Archconfraternity, the principal modifications were more superficial than substantial, carried out by taking few and simple measures: dormitories were created either in the existing large halls or by joining smaller rooms together; the splendid frescoes were covered over; the windows were heightened and provided with grates so that the nuns and orphans were neither able to look out nor be seen from the outside.

The orphan girls, who in 1601 numbered over 150, soon outgrew the structures: before 1616 a new dormitory was constructed above the former right aisle; in 1632 another two were created together with the underlying porticoes on the north and west sides of the first courtyard, of which the one on the west side was obtained by linking the Gothic gallery to the adjoining tower. Again in 1672-73, a completely new building (comprising a portico and a large wash house on the ground floor and two spacious dormitories on the first floor) was added to the south side of the complex. In 1628, also the space destined for the orchard and garden was enlarged on the initiative of Urban VIII.

The works promoted by the Archconfraternity and its cardinal protectors were intermingled with those generously patronized by the titular cardinals. In particular, as regards the basilica, Henry of Portugal had the coffered wood ceilings made in the nave and transept. Between 1621 and 1624, during the pontificate of Urban VIII, the titular cardinal Giovanni Garzia Mellini organized a refurbishment of the presbytery, where he had the apse frescoed by the Florentine painter Giovanni da San Giovanni and transferred the relics placed under the altar by Leo IV into the restored crypt. In 1632, his successor, Girolamo Vidoni, had an altar erected in the left nave containing the head of St Sebastian, discovered among the relics. After 1628, a larger choir was constructed above the portico of the church, for which purpose it was doubled in size.

No significant changes appear to have been made in the 18th century, also as a result of the extreme poverty that prevailed. During this and the following century the number of orphans housed in the complex diminished drastically, also because of the foundation of other welfare institutions. In 1872, the Italian State

Fig. 27. *The interior of the basilica around 1908, with the small windows of the choir gallery still open and the choir stall at the back of the right aisle, where the positive organ can just be seen in the corner (British School at Rome,* Bulwer collection *IV. 4).*

abolished the conservatory of orphan girls and in 1879 divided the complex into two: the west part was allocated to the Augustinian Nuns who still live there to this day, having established a training house on the premises in 1971; the east side was expropriated and initially used as a lazar house, and then from 1910 was entrusted to the Sisters of Our Lady on Mount Calvary to assist deaf-mutes.

In 1946, it was repurchased by the Vatican and since 1995 it has been assigned to the Little Sisters of the Lamb, a community founded in 1983 as a branch of the Order of Preachers.

3.9. Present-day restoration works and discoveries

Since the beginning of the 20th century, the history of the complex has been marked by numerous restoration works aimed at both maintaining its efficiency and enhancing its artistic and historical aspects. The numerous discoveries that have taken place during these works were made possible by the fact that, in the past, the lack of funds on the part of the Archconfraternity as well as the limited interest for a female institution, had impeded any radical transformations of the mediaeval structures, in many cases passed down to us unaltered below thin layers of plaster.

In brief, starting in 1908 until 1916 the Superintendence of Monuments conducted important restoration works thanks to the activities of Antonio Muñoz, who was responsible for numerous other works on famous monuments in Rome. His actions were aimed mainly at recovering the mediaeval aspect of the basilica, the entrance tower and the chapel of St Sylvester.

Other restoration works done by the State Superintendences followed this

Fig. 28. *Gothic hall, view towards north.*

Fig. 29, 30, 31. *The Augustinian Nuns in the basilica during a Solemn Profession of Vows (photo: Augustinian Nuns of Ss. Quattro).*

one, which between 1957 and 1964 involved the consolidation of the apse and the restoration of the former right aisle of the Leonine basilica along with the adjoining chapel, and have in the last fifteen years resulted in many finds of historical and artistic interest, above all that of the frescoes in the Gothic Hall (1995).

Since 1999, instead, an interdisciplinary group of experts supervised by Giovanni Carbonara and directed by the author of this guide has been involved in the restoration of the Cosmati cloister. The archaeological excavations included in the latter (2002-2004) led, among other things, to the discovery of the already mentioned baptistry.

In general, new data emerging in recent years has contributed to underlining the historical and artistic importance of the complex of Santi Quattro Coronati and to illustrating how its vicissitudes are significantly linked to the history of the city of Rome itself. ■

4. The visit

4.1. The entrance façade

The main façade opens onto a small square on Via dei Ss. Quattro and to the east faces San Giovanni in Laterano (*Basilica Salvatoris*), the cathedral church of the city and papal seat until the start of the 15th century. It is the result of a long process of transformation, which involved the entire building complex to the back of the façade, and also comprised the reutilization of structures from the Roman age as foundations. Part of these came to light under the square in 1943 during the construction of a large cistern; part are visible in the basement areas that open onto the road to the right of the façade itself.

The lower section at ground level incorporates the portico of Leo IV. As with all Leonine constructions it was built with bricks, which are clearly visible on the right-hand side, and was pierced at the front by three groups of arches on columns separated by pillars. Evidence of this can be seen to the right, next to the angle buttress, where a semicircular crack follows the line of the first arch. The latter, together with the adjoining arch and a pillar, were left visible in the interior rooms (1995). This reconstruction of the original design of the portico led to its identification in a rare drawing of the late 16th century, in which it is evident that the rhythm created by arches of slightly different dimensions arranged with mirror symmetry was very different to the classical models.

The portico was filled in and raised in the 13th century using *tufelli* (masonry consisting of small rectangular tufa blocks, commonly used in Rome and its surroundings during this period), visible thanks to the plaster losses to the right of the main door, where the *tufelli* alternate with bands of small rough-hewn marble fragments, a construction method that is also present in the first courtyard.

The present configuration of the façade with its plaster surface that conceals the mediaeval structures dates to the 17th century, when orphans were housed

Fig. 32. *The entrance façade with the 18th-century clock on the tower and the quadruple arch openings filled in, in a watercolour of 1833 by Achille Pinelli (Rome, Museo di Roma, n. 4010).*

Fig. 33.
Reconstruction of the porticoed façade of Leo IV (in green) superimposed onto the outline of the existing structure.

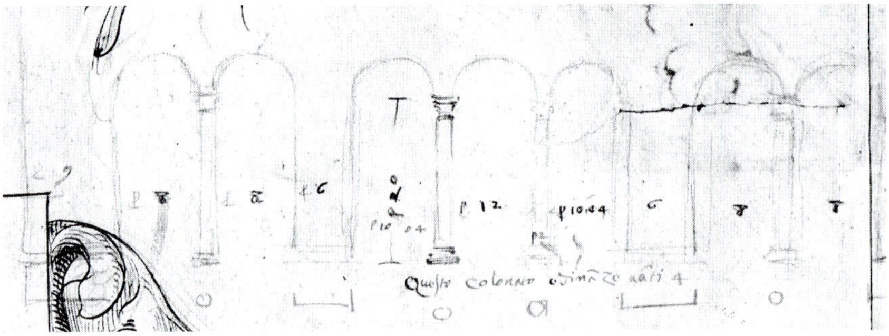

Fig. 34. *Detail of a sheet from a sketchbook of Alberto Alberti (late 16th cent.) with the outline of the Leo IV portico before its modification in the 17th century (Rome, Istituto Nazionale per la Grafica, F.N. 8045, fasc. B,* fol. *35*v, *by kind permission of the Ministry for Cultural Properties and Activities).*

within the complex and, for this reason, the simple rectangular windows protected on the inside by grates were raised to prevent them from looking out.

The only decoration is the fresco, much of which is missing, depicting the Four Saints by the modest painter Pompilio Pizzi in 1690, on the lunette above the portal. The very damaged monochrome painting, which resembles the preparatory design of a palm tree, the symbol of martyrdom, situated to the right of the portal is, instead, of a certain interest as a testimony of devotion.

The façade is dominated by the massive tower constructed by Leo IV on the east wing of the quadriporticus (see later). From the small square we can clearly see the cell, pierced by quadruple arch openings on marble pillars (in the Late Middle Ages the quadruple arches on the south side were replaced by triple arches separated by pillars made of bricks alternating with *tufelli*).

As the numerous traces testify, the tower was covered with plaster frescoed in vivid colours. In particular, the decorations with gems and non-figurative designs that have survived under the quadruple arches on the east side are visible, though with difficulty due to their height.

This tower, unique to Rome, which recalls examples of German origin, was not actually isolated but formed an integral part of the group of buildings constructed by Leo IV in front of the basilica. It must have contained bells, at least

from the Late Middle Ages, but we do not know whether it functioned as a bell tower from the very beginning. In 1769, a clock was installed at the top of the tower with two dial-plates inserted on the east and west sides. It was removed by Antonio Muñoz in 1912, who also reopened the quadruple arches of the cell, which had been partially filled in. The position of the dial-plate is still evident from the outline traced by the differently shaped and coloured brickwork.

Fig. 35. *The quadruple arch opening on the west side of the tower of Leo IV with remains of the original plaster layer around it.*

Fig. 36. *Remains of the fresco decoration of one of the intradoses of the quadruple arch opening on the east side of the tower of Leo IV (photo: L. Barelli).*

4.2. The first courtyard

After passing through the wide corridor that runs under the tower, we enter the first courtyard through a pointed arch. This replaced the quadriporticus of Leo IV, which consisted of an open space of rectangular plan with columned porticoes on all four sides. In order to mentally reconstruct the 9th-century courtyard, the visitor must stretch his/her imagination. The two Leonine wings to the right and at the back were replaced by two 17th-century porticoes of the same length. In place of the left wing, today we find a wider 13th-century construction (the door at the top of the flight of steps provides access to the Convent of the Little Sisters of the Lamb), so that the existing open space is narrower than the former Leonine courtyard. Lastly, the wing on the entrance side is the only one that has been almost entirely preserved, even though it has been filled in and concealed by plaster. If we turn and face the entrance from the centre of the courtyard, we can

Fig. 37. *First courtyard. To the right and at the back, the 17th-century porticoes that replaced the wings of the Leonine quadriporticus. To the left, the 13th-century building enlarged at the time of Cardinal Carrillo (1423-1434).*

Fig. 38. *First courtyard. The east side dominated by the tower of Leo IV.*

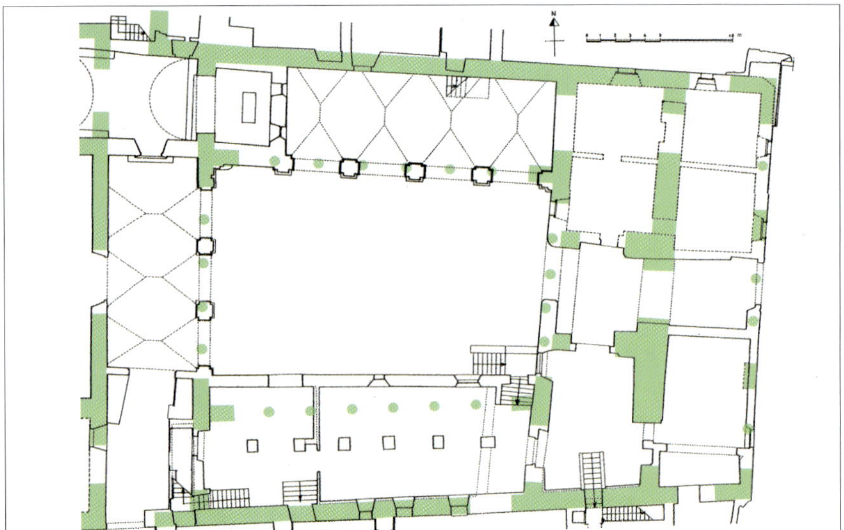

Fig. 39. *Plan of the east section of the complex, with the reconstruction of the 9th-century layout in green.*

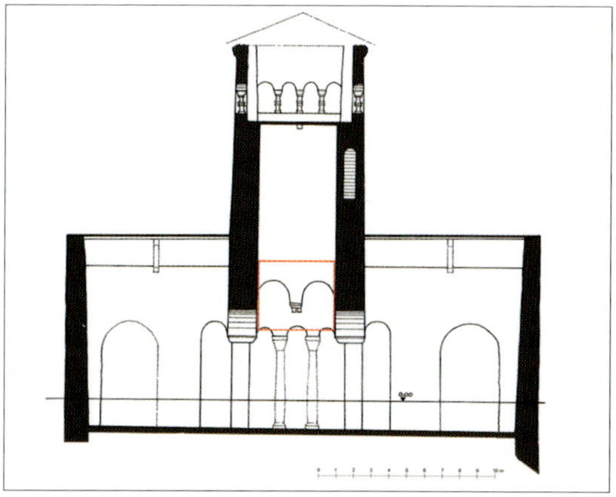

visualize how the tower rose above it and did not take on its present fortified appearance, as its lower section was entirely pierced: the north, east and south sides were opened with wide arches on pillars, while on the west side the three small arches on columns that were linked to two further arches positioned at the sides produced a single porticoed façade. Above, the heavy mass of the tower soaring upwards must, in contrast, have filled the onlooker with wonder. Part of the arches, traces of which can be seen above the entrance arch, have been left exposed on the first floor inside the building in the chapel of the Little Sisters.

For the relatively slender supports to be able to sustain the heavy structure of the tower, certain construction devices were adopted, namely, the tapering of the tower as it rose upwards and the use of masonry with a light and spongy nucleus. In particular, to enable the west wall (1.65 m thick) to rest on three arches, a complex system of corbels was adopted and the corner columns were reinforced at the back by two square pilasters.

Having briefly reconstructed the aspect of the courtyard at the time of Leo IV, we must imagine what became of it in the 13th century following the development of the Cardinal's palace. On the east and west sides the Leonine wings remained. The latter was perhaps filled in and a terrace was almost certainly built above it, which over the course of the century was replaced by a splendid gallery with two

Fig. 40. *Reconstructed elevation, facing west, of the east wing of the Leo IV quadriporticus. The red outline indicates the position of the photograph on the right.*

Fig. 41. *Interior of the tower of Leo IV: view of the structures linking the west wall of the tower to the arches on underlying columns (today the chapel of the Little Sisters of the Lamb).*

Fig. 42. *First courtyard. The room with the two sets of five-light ogival windows (13th cent.) situated above the west portico.*

Fig. 43, 44. *First courtyard. The 13th-century building that replaced the south wing of the Leonine quadriporticus. To the right, detail from the thermographic survey of the wall, which reveals the underlying decoration of alternating bands of* tufelli *and rough-hewn marble fragments.*

sets of five-light ogival windows separated by marble colonnettes with frescoed plant volutes in the intradoses, today revealed within the building.

The original height of the palace, constructed on the south side, roughly corresponds to the first two floors of the existing building. It stood out because of its vividly decorated surface that featured alternating bands of *tufelli* and rough-hewn marble fragments, today only just visible at points where the plaster has disappeared, but confirmed by thermographic surveys. Lastly, on the north side, the Leonine wing, which must have almost totally collapsed, was not reconstructed. The few surviving structures of the north-west corner were incorporated into the presbytery of the St Sylvester chapel on the ground floor of the Great Tower according to Cardinal Stefano Conti's wishes. The external walls of the presbytery, today incorporating the 17th-century porticoes, are recognizable from the brick wall pierced by narrow single windows and oculi, splayed in order to channel the light from above.

On the south wall of the presbytery, we can see the remains of the corner pillar of the Leonine quadriporticus, distinguishable thanks to the chiselled stone surface. Directing our gaze upwards, above the 17th-century porticoes, we can appreciate the stature of the Great Tower with its few openings and high, smooth brick walls with *tufelli* higher up, encircled at the summit by a row of standard holders. The tower has the same essential quality that we find in the more important examples of 13th-century Roman civil architecture, like the Torre dei Conti or the Torre delle Milizie. Originally there was a terrace at the top, from where the rainwater flowed into the cisterns (the present roof dates to 1596).

We owe the subsequent phase of the courtyard to the works of the Spanish cardinal, Alfonso Carrillo, who between 1423 and 1431 dedicated himself to the restoration of the complex, as the inscription in Gothic letters surmounted by his coat-of-arms above the ogival portal testifies. The filling in of the arches of the east wing of the Leonine quadriporticus with the construction of the pointed entrance arch, and the addition of a floor to the building on the south side, where a huge frescoed hall (not open to the public) was created with a frieze of plant motifs inserted into his coat-of-arms within a Gothic compass rose and where on the outside we can see an embedded marble fragment from a double arch opening also bearing his coat-of-arms, can be attributed to his works.

Fig. 45. *First courtyard, west portico. Frescoes depicting the* Birth of the Virgin *and the* Presentation of the Virgin at the Temple, *dated 1588.*

Only in 1632 did the courtyard assume its present aspect: the north and west porticoes were constructed, with two dormitories for the orphans above, one of which was created by linking the Gothic gallery to an adjoining room. As was frequently the case during this period, the plaster on these structures was given an imitation stone treatment, marking the joints of the hewn stone blocks with thin incised lines (these are just visible beneath the modern paintwork, particularly on the first floor pilaster strips).

Continuing our visit, we reach the portico at the back of the courtyard, which rests against the façade of the basilica of Leo IV: the door that leads into the next courtyard is still the central door - its dimensions only slightly modified - of the three doors that coincided with the former Leonine nave and aisles. To the left of the portico is the "door of the carts" that leads into the garden enclosure of the

Fig. 46. *First courtyard, west portico. The portal of the chapel of St Sylvester dated 1570 and the Late Mannerist fresco depicting the Four Saints.*

monastery; to the right, we observe a travertine portal with the inscription STATUARIORUM ET LAPICIDARUM CORPUS MDLXX, surmounted by a Late Mannerist fresco depicting the four martyrs, which leads into the chapel of St Sylvester (see later). This doorway was built by the University of Marble Workers, whose patron saints were the Four Martyrs, in order to enter the chapel without passing through from the nuns' parlour, where the original entrance was located.

We also owe the other interesting Late Mannerist frescoes situated under the portico and dated 1588 to the endeavours of the Marble Workers. They depict two episodes from the *Life of Mary* (*Birth of the Virgin* and *Presentation in the Temple*) divided by gigantic spiral columns. Above, a painted inscription (unfortunately not intact, even though a further fragment is visible from the hall above), recalls the marble workers that commissioned and funded the paintings, and who belonged to the Sernobius and Argentus families of stonemasons of Lombard origin: [...] ANGELUS SERNOBIUS [...]/[...B]ERNAS BARTHO[LOMEUS] ARGENTUS DE VI[...]/[...C]AMERARIUS SUO AERE FACIUNDUM [CU]RARUN[T] 1588. The author of the works is unknown, although they have a certain affinity with the Tuscan painter Giovanni Battista Naldini (c. 1537–1591). The frescoes terminate with a straight line partially interrupted by the existing vaulting, which indicates how the portico was covered by a wooden ceiling before the construction of the vaults in 1632.

4.3. The second courtyard

In the second courtyard, we can better and more easily appreciate the traces of the main transformations of the complex, from Leo IV's reconstruction to the changes carried out to adapt it for use as a conservatory for orphaned girls.

As already mentioned, the space comprising the courtyard coincides with the eastern half of the nave of the Leonine basilica that, in its turn, corresponds to the space occupied by the 4th-century hall, whose walls are clearly visible in the underlying rooms. The entrance side of the courtyard is therefore none other than the façade of the Leonine basilica that has been preserved up to a considerable height. On it, we can note traces of the lower sections of three windows that illuminated the nave, just visible below the roof line, and the remains of a marble cornice made with pieces of recovered Roman stone, which divided the façade in two and originally continued along the whole length of the nave: in particular, in the right corner on entering we see two corbels that support a slab bearing a male bust.

The lateral walls of the courtyard replace the arcades that delineated the nave. In the corner of the left wall closest to the entrance a protruding pillar supports a frag-

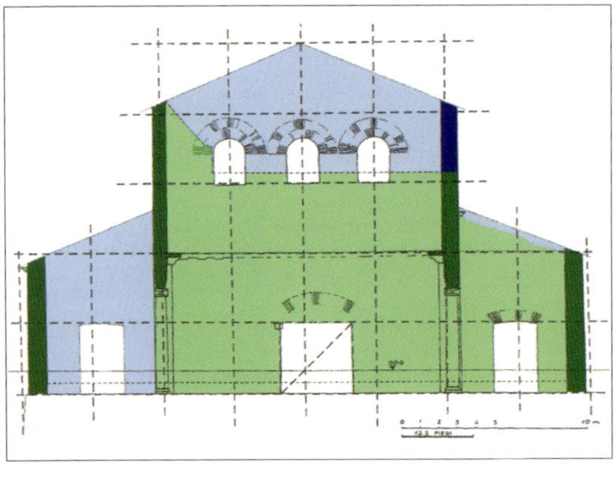

Fig. 47. *Reconstruction of the elevation of the basilica of Leo IV looking towards the back of the entrance façade: in green, the preserved, in blue, the demolished sections. The superimposed dotted lines indicate the geometrical plan based on a modular grid of 12.5 feet (385 cm).*

Fig. 48. *Second courtyard. Remains of the Leonine cornice of the former nave made with marble fragments from the Roman age.*

Fig. 49. *Second courtyard. The south wall with the remains of the architrave of the former nave (indicated by the arrow).*

ment of broken architrave; evidence that the arcades on either side of the Leonine basilica were surmounted by a marble architrave that terminated precisely on this pillar. After the restoration works of the basilica - partially burnt down by the Normans - were interrupted without reconstructing the section of arcade coinciding with this wall, the architrave fragment that had remained *in situ* was incorporated in the 12th

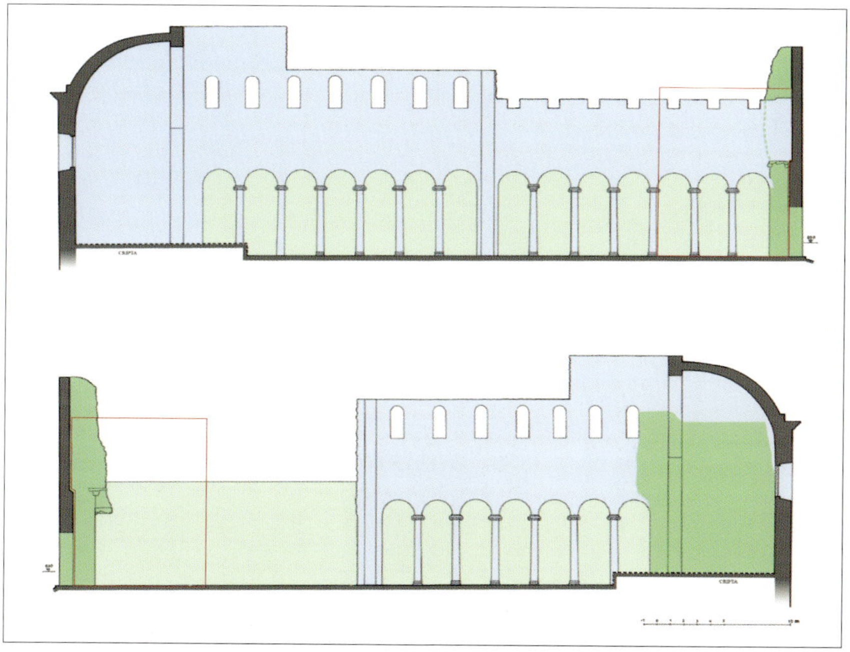

Fig. 50. *Reconstructed elevations indicating the state of the construction site for the restoration of the basilica desired by Pascal II at the moment the works were interrupted (in green, the sections preserved from the Leonine age; in blue, the sections reconstructed by Pascal II; the red outlines correspond to the photographed sections in fig. 51 and 49.*

Fig. 51. *Second courtyard. The north wall with the arcades and overlying windows created by Pascal II, filled in during the 13th century.*

Fig. 52. *The portico of Pascal II in a 16th-century engraving from [Fra Santi Solinori],* Le cose maravigliose dell'alma città di Roma... rappresentate in disegno da Gieronimo Francino..., *Venice 1588.*

Fig. 53. *Second courtyard. The west wall with the portico in front of the church and the overlying nuns' choir, constructed in the first half of the 17th century.*

century into a new wall that delineated the rooms of the Benedictine monastery. From the right side of the courtyard, instead, it is possible to see how the Leonine pilaster, symmetrical to the one just mentioned (distinguishable from the rest of the wall by its less regular masonry), was reutilized at the start of the series of arches on columns with Ionic capitals, constructed to replace those of Pascal II, when he initially attempted to restore the basilica of Leo IV. On looking closer, we can also distinguish the lower limits of the windows that surmounted the arches, later filled in and replaced by the present 17th-century ones. Looking upwards, it is also possible to see how these structures directly supported the more imposing ones of the Great Tower.

Fig. 54. *Second courtyard. The* trompe l'oeil *entrance portal to the basilica and detail of the central panel with the depiction of the orphan girls and nuns venerating the Four Saints.*

Fig. 55. *Second courtyard. Detail of one of the frescoed intradoses.*

The arches were progressively filled in during the 13th century in order to create additional rooms in the Cardinal's palace, but first the intradoses were decorated with frescoes, partly made visible in modern times by opening the upper lunettes of the arches. The most preserved intrados shows a motif of coloured flower volutes on a white ground, which does not seem too far removed from the other 13th-century decorations. In the filled-in section of the second arch on the right, we find the door to the *Calendar* room (see later), which is the entrance to the parlour of the Augustinian monastery and from where it is possible to visit the chapel of St Sylvester (ring bell).

Lastly, the wall at the back of the courtyard is that of the new façade constructed by Pascal II to reduce the size of the basilica, almost totally concealed by the deep portico on two floors that precedes it. This consists of two rows each with three spans, covered by cross vaults supported at the sides by pillars and at the centre by four columns. The area on the upper floor contains the nuns' choir.

This portico is also the result of successive transformations: the bays closest to the church correspond to a first portico constructed by Pascal II, above which one of the three galleries that overlooked the nave (see later) was originally positioned. It was made up of three arches supported at each end by two pillars and in the centre by two columns with Ionic angular capitals, still in existence today. The latter were subsequently reinforced at the back by square pilasters before 1588, the year in which an engraving already illustrates them.

Pascal II's portico was doubled in size after 1628 in order to create the choir on the first floor. In completing this operation, we can see how two late Renaissance windows present on the left side of the courtyard were partially obliterated.

Under the portico, we reach the door to the basilica surrounded by a *trompe l'oeil* with columns and a curvilinear tympanum, interrupted at the centre by an aedicule, in which the Augustinian Nuns and orphaned girls are depicted while they venerate the patron saints. To the right of the door an inscription records the restoration works completed in 1914 by Antonio Muñoz and next to it a square patch in the plaster layer reveals the masonry of Pascal II's façade. Two broken sections of large pink granite columns stand on either side of the entrance, placed there by Muñoz, who discovered them when excavating the crypt.

4.4. The church

4.4.1. The interior

On entering the door we are confronted with a view of the whole interior of the basilica, which is essentially that consecrated by Pascal II in 1116: a space with a nave and two aisles, the latter surmounted by galleries, concluding with a high transept that leads into the great apse. The aisles are separated from the nave by two rows of

Fig. 56. *Interior of the basilica looking towards the apse.*

four columns with Corinthian and Composite capitals. At the front of the nave, the final arches of the arcades rest on the two large rectangular pillars supporting the triumphal arch that opens into the transept. A triforium-arcade comprising two sets of triple arches separated by smaller columns, with Ionic capitals and parapets of marble, surmounts the nave-arcades and originally allowed one to look down from the galleries. A further triforium-arcade, whose remains are still visible on the back of the façade, coincided with a third gallery situated above the entrance portico.

The present space is the result of the reduction in size desired by Pascal II: the new perimeter was determined to the west by the old apse, to the north and south by the arcades of the former nave belonging to Pascal II's attempt to restore the Leonine basilica, and to the east by a completely new façade erected just in front of the cruciform pilasters that marked the halfway point of the former building. Along the walls of the aisles it is possible to see the pilasters and columns left partially exposed following the restoration works of the early 20th century.

The fact that the church was inserted within the pre-existing nave explains some of its architectonic peculiarities, such as the disproportionate width of the

Fig. 57. *Interior of the basilica looking towards the back of the entrance façade on which the remains of the triforium-arcade of the east gallery can be seen.*

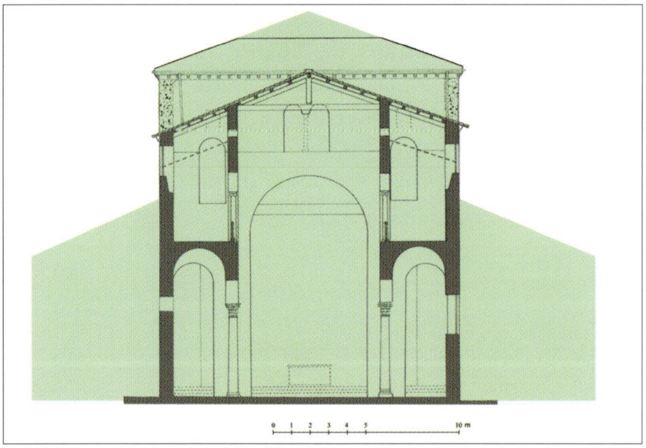

Fig. 58. *Reconstructed elevation of the basilica reduced in size by Pascal II (in green, the space occupied by the Leonine basilica after the attempt to restore it following the fire of 1084; the dotted lines indicate the roof according to the first project to reduce the size).*

Fig. 59. *The coffered wood ceiling with the coat-of-arms of Henry, King of Portugal (1547-1580) at the centre.*

Fig. 60. *Detail of the Cosmati pavement with the quincunx motif at the centre.*

apse that, in an anomalous way, coincides with all three aisles, and how the presence of the galleries that, though unusual for the period, turned out to be a sensible way of exploiting the considerable height of the walls.

The configuration of the upper part of the aisles was also influenced by the preexisting structures. An initial project envisaged a basilica plan for the church, with a higher nave illuminated by oculi above the galleries. The façade, which in the part extending above the portico was framed by pilaster strips and capped by a brick cornice with saw-tooth edging, was erected according to plan. In order to complete the whole project, however, it would be necessary to demolish the higher sections of the walls of the former nave. Instead, with the works almost at their conclusion, it was decided to leave the walls intact and cover the three aisles with a double-pitched roof. To do this, the space lying between the high part of the façade of the new nave and the side walls of the former nave, which went as far as including the windows, was walled up. The latter were partially filled in and help to illuminate the galleries directly. The walls of the new basilica were lastly capped by a cornice made with marble corbels recovered from the Leonine church and projecting bricks.

In the west sector of the basilica, which is the part today that, compared to Pascal II's church, has undergone greater transformations, the pope had the presbytery floor raised a few steps higher, at the front of which doors opened onto the steps leading down to the crypt of Leo IV. He had the steps reconstructed parallel to the walls of the transept, rotating them therefore 90° with respect to the original ones located in the former aisles that, with the reduction in size of the

Fig. 61. *Antonio Eclisse, copy of the lost fresco of the* Crucifixion *formerly situated on the back of the entrance façade, commissioned by Divitia and dated 1248 (Vienna, Österreichische Nationalbibliothek,* Cod. Ser. nov. *3311, fol. 36).*

church, had become inaccessible. Above the presbytery the pope then had a new altar constructed, surmounted by a ciborium, and lastly, he introduced new liturgical fittings. Few of these remain, among them several small pilasters today in the cloister (similar to those used at S. Maria in Cosmedin, reconsecrated in 1123), and the marble frontal of the high altar (see later).

Since the time of Pascal II, the beautiful Cosmati mosaic pavement (the term derives from the name of the sculptor-architect families, the Cosmati, who worked in Rome between the 12th and 13th centuries, although many works thus described were actually made by other artists) that embellishes the interior has been preserved. The most precious part of the decoration is that running along the central axis of the basilica, consisting of a series of *rotae* (large stone discs typical of this type of paving), culminating at the centre of the nave with the largest *rota* made of porphyry, inserted between four smaller discs positioned symmetrically at the sides in a quincunx motif. Ancient marbles were reused in the pavement, among them many stone tablets with inscriptions coming from the catacombs, the most important of which were removed and displayed on the walls of the crypt in 1880 and in the cloister during the 1911-1914 restoration.

The fresco that covered the vault of the apse, commissioned during the pontificate of Pascal II by a devotee named *Tuttabona* and executed by two artists who sign themselves *G. G. et Petrolinus Pictores,* was, instead, completely lost. This was how the painter Guilio Mancini described it just before its destruction in 1621: "The style is extremely good, the feet stand on the surfaces, which in these times and also in later times we have not seen standing so convincingly. The drapery is very well interpreted, not like it was in the age of Cimabue. This painting is worth seeing for the apparel of the Martyrs and virgins, both the males and females, with the diadem similar to a frontlet, and for the pontifical vestments of those times". Perhaps a frieze frescoed above the apsidal arch, visible in the loft area, belongs to this decorative scheme.

The most important transformations of Pascal II's basilica, apart from the insertion of the side altars and the changes to the presbytery (see later), were the construction of the coffered wood ceilings financed by the titular cardinal Henry, King of Portugal (1547-1580), whose carved coat-of-arms appears on the ceiling at the centre of the nave, and the creation of a larger choir obtained by doubling the size of the external portico (after 1628), as well as the small choirs that replaced the galleries. In order to complete the latter, the barrel vaults that covered the aisles were replaced with cross vaults at a lower height. Small windows protected by grates were opened (later filled in during the 1911-1914 restoration) below the triforium-arcade, so that the nuns and orphans were able to attend the religious functions without being seen.

4.4.2. Traces of mediaeval fresco decoration

In the area closest to the entrance, there are significant examples of the fresco decorations applied to the perimeter walls of the basilica during the Middle Ages. These are votive panels, as indicated by their depiction of certain donors or of their coat-of-arms, which were whitewashed over in 1673 and brought to light again in

Fig. 62. *Detail of the 14th-century frescoes of the right aisle, from right to left: the lower half of a saint, St Bartholomew, a bishop saint, St Benedict with the donor (a monk) kneeling in the foreground.*

Fig. 63. *Detail of the 13th-century frescoes on the back of the entrance façade: a monk in discussion with* Magister Rainaldus.

the early 20th century. The decoration was originally more widespread: on the back of the entrance façade, for example, there used to be a *Crucifixion* (dated 1248 and known to us from engravings) and a *Madonna with Angels*, commissioned respectively by a devotee by the name of Divitia and another by the name of Maria.

To the right entering the church, on the back of the entrance façade, St Antony is represented with two saints, one of which can be identified as Catherine of Alexandria from the wheel held in her hand, the symbol of her martyrdom. They continue on the long wall of the aisle, after the cruciform pilaster revealed thanks to the removal of the plaster layer, from right to left: 1) the *Pietà of Christ* portrayed between two angels with Sts Peter and Paul at the sides; 2) panel of St Bartholomew, recognizable from the skin stripped from him during his martyrdom, which hangs from his shoulder, and a saint without his upper half; 3) panel with a bishop saint and St Benedict (truncated on the left by the altar positioned there at a later date) with the monk who commissioned it at his feet; 4) after the altar that has obviously concealed some of the decoration, a panel depicts the protomartyrs St Lawrence and St Stephen. These frescoes, dating to the 14th century, share similarities with others present in the monasteries of Subiaco in that they both appear to be influenced by the Sienese School. On the opposite side of the basilica, the pilaster strip on the back of the façade in line with the arcade depicts a pope saint (Gregory the Great?); below him, a panel with two monks in discussion: under the right figure we can still read the name *MAG[ISTER] RAINALD[US]*. Continuing along the back wall of the façade coinciding with the left aisle, the upper register depicts from left to right: St Augustine, and after the single window, three seated saints; in the lower register, a *Scene of Martyrdom*, much of which has been lost. On the adjoining wall above the confessional box, we find the *Church Censer* and again a saint on the cruciform pilaster. Dating the frescoes on this side is more difficult because of their poor state of repair and due to the fact that the higher part was probably repainted in the 17th century (a continuous line, added during restoration, marks the extent of the original part). The panel with the two monks dates to around the mid-13th century.

4.4.3. The monuments of the right aisle

The columns with Ionic capitals of Pascal II's arches belonging to the former nave, left partially exposed, follow each other along the right wall of the basilica. We can observe that the column closest to the altar is higher and rests directly on the pavement of the Leonine church, which has been left visible inside a pit, 55 cm lower than the existing floor.

At the centre of the aisle, we find the late Renaissance Altar of the Manger with an elaborate stucco frame and a splendid altarpiece depicting the *Mystery of the Birth of Jesus*, in the manner of Zuccaro (c. 1585). To the left of the altar a window, whose jambs consist of early mediaeval marble decorations, had been opened within the filled-in arch of Pascal II.

Fig. 64. *Right aisle. Altar of the Manger (late 16th cent.).*

Fig. 65. *Right aisle. Altar of the Crucifixion (early 17th cent.).*

Fig. 66, 67. *Right aisle. Altar of the Crucifixion (early 17th cent.), detail of the face of the Madonna before the 1995 restoration (above, photo: L. Barelli) and after (below).*

Proceeding forwards, we find the monument dedicated to Monsignor Luigi d'Aquino, auditor general of the Apostolic Chamber, benefactor of the orphan girls, who died in 1679. Made with polychrome marbles, it bears a black stone commemorative plaque in the centre with the coat-of-arms of the defunct below, and above, an urn with two rampant lions similar to those depicted in the coat-of-arms; in the upper part, a bust of the defunct in an oval niche is surmounted by a cross. An inscription on the pavement lies above the place of interment. Against the right pillar of the triumphal arch we have the Altar of the Crucifixion. Originally dedicated to St Lawrence, it was installed at the request of the titular cardinal Lorenzo Pucci (1513-1524, but died in 1531). The 17th-century fresco above the mensa portrays Christ on the Cross with the Virgin, St John the Baptist, Mary Magdalen and, kneeling in the foreground, the two protomartyrs St Lawrence and St Stephen. The Madonna is depicted as being elderly and this was not appreciated, so much so that a younger face was later painted over her in oils, removed during the 1995 restoration.

4.4.4. The monuments of the left aisle

Only two of the columns from Pascal II's restoration of the great basilica are visible along the left wall, one of which stands on the pavement constructed during this phase, left visible about 18 cm below the present paving.

On the long wall of the aisle next to the wood confessional is the foundling wheel through which the nuns passed the sacred vessels in church. The Altar of the Annunciation follows, dating to around 1623-24. The altar itself is a solid block of marble, probably early mediaeval, adorned by a bas-relief cross, on which the marble mensa lies. The grate above, surmounted by a stucco panel framing a fresco of the *Annunciation* by Giovanni da San Giovanni (see later), allowed the

Fig. 68. *Left aisle. Altar of the Annunciation (c. 1623-24).*

nuns and orphans to venerate the Altar of the Manger situated on the opposite side without leaving the cloister. On the ground to the left of the altar lies the ledger stone of the Portuguese cardinal, Ordonho Alvarez, who died in 1285, with his coat-of-arms repeated twice. At the centre of the wall of the left aisle stands the most venerated altar of the basilica. It is dedicated to St Sebastian and contains his head. The precious relic was discovered by Cardinal Mellini in 1624 among those in the crypt (see later), hidden in a precious silver-gilt vase with niello inlay (today in the Museum of Sacred Art at the Vatican) dating from the inscription to the time of Pope Gregory IV (827-844). Leo IV supposedly placed the head in the crypt, perhaps not by chance, given that the martyr was linked to the legend of the patron saints.

Fig. 69. *Left aisle. Altar of St Sebastian (1632).*

Cardinal Mellini extracted the vase with the head from the other relics with the intention of placing it in a separate altar, but his aim was only fulfilled by his successor Girolamo Vidoni. The latter had the altar built in 1632, as the inscription in gold letters on black marble testifies, and had the relic placed in a niche located above the mensa, protected by a grate, in its turn originally covered by another decorative grate of gilded bronze adorned with angels' heads, stolen in 2001. The

Fig. 70, 71. *Left aisle. Altar of Saints Peter and Paul (early 17th cent.) and detail of the ciborium from the time of Innocent VIII (1484-1492) reused at the centre.*

altar, still stylistically close to late 16th-century examples, was built entirely with precious marbles, among them the two portasanta marble columns on the left and right originating from the ciborium of Pascal II. Above the niche is an altarpiece depicting *St Sebastian cared for by Lucina and Irene*, painted for Cardinal Vidoni by Giovanni Baglione (1571-1644). The altar is completed by the imitation drapery painted on the wall at each side; two angels are also depicted to its left. In 1757, thanks to an iron door, the niche was made accessible from the wall behind it inside the cloister, which permitted the nuns to venerate and maintain the relic.

Immediately to the right of the altar, the carved wooden door leads into the Cosmati cloister (ring bell during opening hours). Above the door lies a marble inscription recalling the generosity of Dorotea Bonfilioli (d. 1652), who left her estate to the orphans. We then find the memorial tablet of Pietro Respighi, titular cardinal of the basilica and Vicar General of His Holiness, who died in 1913 and was transferred here in 1933, and that of his nephew Monsignor Carlo Respighi, rector of the basilica and Prefect of the Apostolic Ceremonies, who died in 1957, both benefactors of the monastery. Their bodies lie together in a burial vault positioned under the pavement, accessible via a circular stone entrance in the floor in front of the cloister door. A small column with its capital and base carved out of one single piece of marble stands below the memorial tablets; it dates to the 9th century and therefore probably belonged to the liturgical fittings of Leo IV. At the head of the nave, the Altar of Sts Peter and Paul (existing in 1628 and restored in 1993-94) stands against the left pillar of the triumphal arch, symmetrical to the Altar of the Crucifixion. The mensa is surmounted by a precious marble ciborium with the coat-of-arms of Innocent VIII (1484-1492), in which four angels carved in bas-relief surround the golden door bearing the image of the Redeemer. This is attributed to Andrea Bregno or to his school or to Luigi Capponi. In the 17th century, two Apostles were painted at the sides, and above, the Eternal Father surrounded by Angels.

4.4.5. The transept and apse

The transept was obtained by reusing the high walls of the former nave, the width of which it therefore maintains. The filled-in arches deprived of their columns are visible on its walls and on the left side also two windows, the only ones not to be walled in or reduced in size, would appear to belong to Pascal II's phase of the great basilica. At the ends of the two aisles we find the steps that lead down to the crypt and the choir stalls where the Augustinian nuns say their daily prayers.

The wood coffered ceiling features a panel depicting the Four Saints. The pavement, like that of the nave, dates to the works of Pascal II: at the centre, there are three rectangular panels containing the characteristic *rotae* and a modern grate that permits access to a part of the crypt (see later); in the areas to the sides, paved with recovered Roman marble slabs and Cosmati mosaic squares (the majority of it dismantled and reconstructed by Muñoz), there are ledger stones from the modern era, among them that of Niccolò Alemanni, Prefect of the Vatican Library, a devotee of this site who died in 1626. The door on the left wall of the transept leads to the sacristy. This is situated in the north-west corner of the cloister; it has a domical vault adorned with 19th-century tempera paintings and here we also find a marble basin placed inside a 15th-century aedicule, with a Cosmati fascia at its base.

On the right wall, another door leads into the nuns' refectory (not open to the public) obtained from the former right aisle of Leo IV's basilica, where it is possible to admire the series of arches on columns constructed by Pascal II in place of the Leonine arcade and some 19th-century remains of mosaic pavement with large tesserae, inserted into the modern paving. The chapel of St Nicholas opens onto the refectory: this was one of the oratories of the Leonine basilica, symmetrical to the chapel of St Barbara, and originally identical in shape to the latter (see later). It had already

Fig. 72. *Giovanni da San Giovanni, vault of the apse,* Glory of all the Saints *(1623).*

Fig. 73. *Interior of the refectory, former right aisle of the Leonine basilica, with the Romanic arches filled in to reduce the size of the church at the time of Pascal II (1099-1118).*

Fig. 74. *Interior of the Chapel of St Nicholas (9th cent.), restored in the 1960s.*

On the following page, above:
Fig. 75. *Francesco Solario da Caronno, stucco angel situated on the right pier of the apsidal arch (1623).*

Fig. 76. *Detail of an element from a Cosmati liturgical fixture (12th-13th cent.) inserted into the pavement of the apse reconstructed in 1624.*

been transformed in the Early Middle Ages perhaps by inserting a cupola and was subsequently further tampered with. The present arrangement of the presbytery dates to the radical works financed by Cardinal Giovanni Garzia Mellini between 1621 and 1624. These consisted of the construction of the roof and the interior decoration of the apse, the excavation beneath the altar to retrieve the relics, the layout of the crypt, the rebuilding of the altar (later dismantled and reassembled by Muñoz), some marble balustrades, and the cardinal's throne. Mellini was also responsible for the present pavement of the apse, into which mediaeval liturgical elements adorned with Cosmati mosaics were inserted. The interior wall of the apse was divided up by fluted pilaster strips of a Corinthian order standing on a high stylobate, and the intercolumnar surfaces, divided into compartments by white and gilt stucco frames, were frescoed by Giovanni da San Giovanni (San Giovanni Valdarno 1592 - Florence 1636) with the stories of the two groups of patron saints. In the lower register we find seven episodes narrating the lives of the five Pannonian martyrs: (from left to right) *Claudius converts Simplicitus*; *Simplicitus is baptized by Bishop Cyril in prison*; *Diocletian gives orders to carve the statue of Asclepius*; *The stonemasons are led to their martyrdom*; *Flagellation with 'scorpiones'*; *The widow of Lampadius demands their death*; *Nicetius drops the stonemasons enclosed in lead boxes into the river*. In the upper register, instead, the story of the four Roman soldiers is narrated in as many episodes alternating with the windows: *The soldiers refuse to offer sacrifice to the god Asclepius; Flagellation with whips armed with lead balls; The bodies are offered to the dogs; St Sebastian and Pope Melchiades bury the bodies on Via Labicana.* Lastly, between the bases of the pilasters, monochrome fresco decorations, much of which has either faded or vanished, illustrate the restoration phases of Mellini. On the piers of the apsidal arch, as well as the stucco angels, frescoes depict the Four Saints with the palm of martyrdom; lower down, two stone inscriptions record the works of Leo IV, Pascal II and Cardinal Mellini. High up on the sides of the apsidal arch are the allegorical figures of *Faith* (left) and *Fortitude* (right). The painted vault depicts the *Glory of all the*

Saints, dominated above by the figures of Christ and God the Father, with the Holy Spirit on high, and immediately below those of the Virgin and St John.

The projection of the elaborate gilded stucco cornice that divides the lower zone of the apse from the vault hides the signatures of the painter and stucco-worker from the observer: GIO[VANNI] DE S[ANCT]O GIO[VAN]NI TOSCHANO FECIT 1623 e FR[ANCES]CO SOLARIO DI CHARONNO STUCCHATORE FECIT A[NN]O 1623.

Fig. 77. *Altar-frontal of Pascal II, today displayed on the left wall of the transept.*

Fig. 78. *The Cardinal's throne (1623-1624).*

Fig. 79. *The 17th-century positive organ.*

The frescoes testify to the development of Giovanni who fuses Florentine, Roman and Emilian culture, and also demonstrates his appreciation of Caravaggesque naturalism. The fresco of the vault, which dominates the entire space of the church diffusing it with a soft and golden light, is remarkable. Its decorative scheme, which recalls perhaps more that of a cupola than of a bowl-shaped vault, comprises a throng of saints represented from below rising upwards with great realism, placed carefully on overlapping layers of clouds. The spatial illusionism created by the positioning and comportment of the figures is enhanced by the progressive reduction of their dimensions, the softening of the outlines and the gradual increase in light as it proceeds upwards. Again Mellini is responsible for placing Pascal II's altar-frontal - at the centre of which perhaps Giovanni da San Giovanni painted a fresco of a Madonna - on the left wall close to the steps leading to the crypt, and on the opposite wall, for the addition of a stone inscription, formerly incomplete and later reintegrated, containing the epitaph poem written by Pope Damasus (366-384) in honour of the martyrs Protus and Hyacinth, originating from the Cemetery of

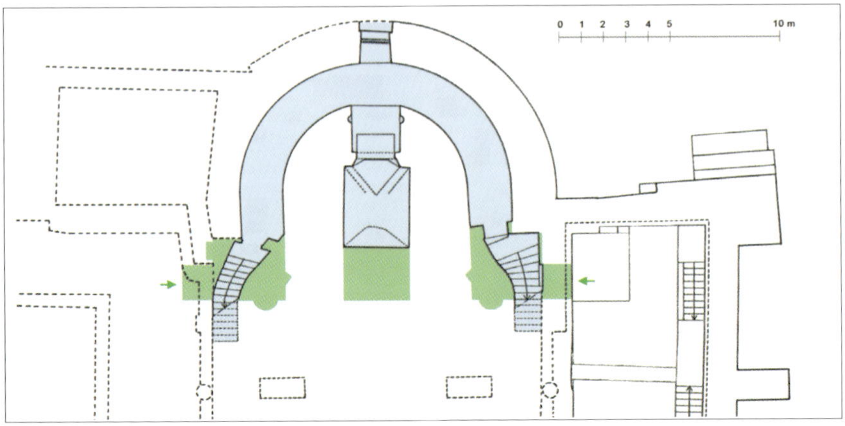

Fig. 80. *Plan of the crypt (in blue, the existing state dating to the works of Cardinal Mellini; in green, the parts that were eliminated from the original configuration).*

St Hermes on *Via Salaria Vetus*. The latter, which was discovered upside down in the pavement, had perhaps arrived at the basilica at the time of Leo IV together with the head of Protus that can be found among the relics in the crypt.

In the apse to the right there is a small 17th-century positive organ, a rare example of a type of portable instrument that, at one time, was very common. The wood exterior is decorated with plant motifs and by a painting of St Cecilia who plays while an angel accompanies her with a lute.

4.4.6. The crypt

The crypt (open on 8 November) was originally of the so-called semi-annular type, that is, formed by a corridor that follows the contours of the apse. Access is gained from the steps located in the side aisles, and from the short corridor that runs at right angles to the centre of the curve to the, often inaccessible, cell designed for the relics, positioned under the high altar. This format was adopted during the Early Middle Ages particularly in Rome, but also in the rest of Italy and Europe, for the purpose of holding relics of saints and martyrs. Its success was ensured by the fact of there being such an illustrious example: the crypt that Gregory the Great (590-604) constructed in the basilica of St Peter's at the Vatican for the purpose of celebrating mass directly above the tomb of the apostle. This one on the Caelian Hill was built by Leo IV for the veneration of the relics that he had placed under the altar in four great Roman baths, arranged one above the other in two pairs, one made of serpentine, one of bronze and two of porphyry.

The crypt underwent its first important transformation under Pascal II who moved the access steps to the sides of the transept. The pope also had the area under the altar excavated to search for the relics, but found only the two upper baths. In 1624, Cardinal Mellini likewise conducted excavations under the altar, and this time discovered all four baths. He then replaced them in the crypt that he had reduced to its present size, by moving the cell to the west and filling in the

Fig. 81. *Crypt. The cell with the baths containing the relics, restored by Cardinal Mellini in 1624.*

east side of the original space (in 1913 this was brought to light by Antonio Muñoz and a grate was placed in the floor of the transept to enable inspection).

Descending the steps to the right of the transept, we see traces of one of the two original doors that gave access to the crypt from the former aisles, and the remains of a fresco of imitation hanging drapery.

At the bottom of each flight of steps, an iron gate protects the entrance that leads into the semi-annular corridor, covered by a lowered barrel vault. Some fragmented stone inscriptions are displayed on the outer wall, some of which were removed from the pavement in 1880. The central part of the curve, where there is a recessed rectangular window protected by a marble lattice-moulding, is covered by a cross vault decorated with 17th-century stuccoes and frescoed with the images of the four *cornicularii,* attributed to Giovanni da San Giovanni. The small corridor starts here: the first section has been transformed into a chapel; this is covered by a barrel vault and also decorated with 17th-century stuccoes with the fresco of God the Father at the centre, likewise attributed to Giovanni. The marble altar at the back is surmounted by a grate, through which it is possible to see the poignant interior of the cell with the four baths containing the relics. The larger bath, of bronze, has been raised on a mound (not visible) where the pious stonemason wrote in rough lettering: DÌ 26 OTOBRE/ MASTRO ANTONIO/ PALIARO FECIT ANNO/ DOMINI 1624.

Fig. 82. *Plan of the area of the Benedictine monastery (in green, the structures of the Leonine basilica; in yellow, the cloister space in the 12th century; the dotted lines indicate the position of the baptistry, today buried).*

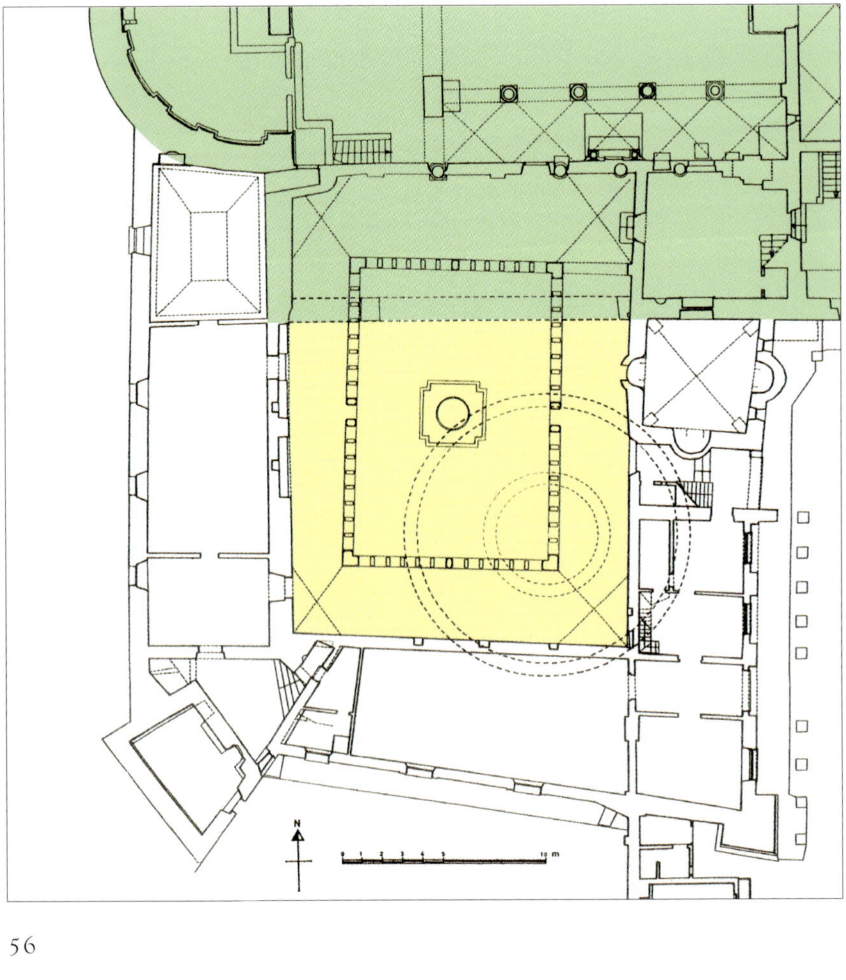

4.5. The area of the Benedictine monastery

4.5.1. The Cosmati cloister

We enter the cloister from the left aisle of the basilica. Archaeological excavations have revealed that, before that of today, another cloister existed on a square plan backing directly onto the outer wall of the former nave of the Leonine basilica, dating to the early 13th century. This must have been the heart of the Benedictine monastery founded by Pascal II, subsequently passed on to the monks of Sassovivo. Within a monastic settlement the cloister, in fact, represented both an essential space for strolling, prayer and aesthetic elevation in that it was a symbol of the garden of paradise, as well as a means of communication around which the church and other buildings that formed part of religious life were distributed. This first cloister, together with the wall of the basilica on which it rested, was demolished at the time the present cloister was built, and perhaps at the same moment also the building on the west wing was constructed, in which it is possible to recognize, due to an analogous situation at Sassovivo, the *palatium dormidorii* that contained the monks' cells.

The 13th-century cloister occupied an area slightly trapezoidal in shape of about 16 x 23 m. It consisted of four corridors, originally only on one level and was covered by a wood roof, arranged around an open cultivated garden area. It was, we might say, 'dropped' into a previously determined space, which would explain the somewhat irregular plan of the corridors, while the central section, constructed with great care in a single phase, forms an almost perfect rectangle in plan consisting of

Fig. 83. *The 13th-century Cosmati cloister viewed from the north corridor after the restoration of the garden in 2005 (sponsor: Robert Wilson).*

Fig. 84. *Cloister. The north corridor after the partial restoration of 2007 (sponsor: Robert Wilson): to the right, the columns of the arcades of the first Romanic basilica filled in by Pascal II (1099-1118) to reduce the church to its existing size.*

walls pierced by small arches resting on ninety-six coupled colonnettes and ten marble pillars positioned at the corners and at the centre of each wing. In the north wing, close to the entrance, in fact, the cloister occupies part of the left aisle of the Leonine basilica. While the position of the external wall of the former aisle is indicated only by the two low sections of modern brickwork, one positioned in the cloister garden close to the north-west corner and the other against the east wall near the chapel of St Barbara (see later), it is quite clear that the arcade that divided this aisle from the nave of the great basilica is now the north wall of the cloister. It is equally evident that the west wall has incorporated the large brick arches dating to before the construction of the *palatium dormidorii* and the cloister itself, as well as

Fig. 85. *Cloister. The west corridor.*

the ancient head of the former Leonine nave. Lastly, the west side of the chapel of St Barbara is incorporated into the centre of the east wall.

The style of the cloister can be described by the term in Roman mediaeval art known as Cosmati. We note the elegance of the decorative details in which diverse cultural and stylistic components are evident, fused into a single harmonious whole: the stiff-leaf coupled capitals and bases, also these paired with protective carved foliage, would seem to point to a Burgundian ancestry. The pillars are decorated with fluted and reeded pilaster strips of a clearly classical derivation. Other elements, instead, uphold the Roman mediaeval tradition: the arched lintel of the small arches; the cornice consisting of alternating rows of projecting bricks with a row of saw-tooth edging above and below the centre row of marble corbels evenly spaced by small squares of Cosmati mosaic; as well as the use of ancient recovered Roman marble, among them fragments of stone inscriptions and architectonic decorations. Lastly, the intradoses bear a decoration carried out during the 1912-16 restoration, based on two fragments with the original frescoed design, one with black and white triangles (north wing), and the other with green and red drops (east wing).

Of particular interest are the remains of colouring on the cornice, which was covered by a thin layer of plaster frescoed with a red colour imitating that of terracotta, apart from the corbels and the horizontal surfaces, which were both painted white to imitate marble. Furthermore, considering that the remaining masonry surfaces of the cloister were painted with red bricks, alternating with thick layers of white mortar (what is defined as *falsa cortina* pointing, prevalent in Rome during the 12th and 13th centuries), we can assume that, also in this case, the original aspect of the cloister was very different to what it is today.

There are evident links between the 13th-century cloisters in Rome and Lazio, like those for example of S. Sabina (later than 1222) and S. Cosimato (c. 1247) in Rome, S. Scolastica at Subiaco (constructed in Rome and assembled *in situ* between 1220 and 1243), or the richer and more complex cloisters of S. Giovanni in Laterano (1216-1230) and S. Paolo fuori le Mura (c. 1208-1230). As regards the precise dating and the name of the author, it is possible to form some hy-

Fig. 86. *Cloister. Detail of the Cosmati cornice after its restoration in 2002.*

Fig. 87. *The cloister in 1912 before the restoration works of Antonio Muñoz (from Muñoz,* Il restauro, *p. 88).*

potheses thanks to the comparison with the cloister at the Sassovivo abbey. Part of the latter was built by the Roman marble worker Petrus de Maria, who carved the pieces in Rome and delivered them to none other than the monastery of Ss. Quattro, from where they were taken to Sassovivo to be assembled. The works were still in progress in 1233. The differences between the two cloisters are substantial, but the analogies that exist are also surprising. We can therefore reasonably assume that Petrus de Maria was one, if not the only one, of the artists involved in the execution of the Roman cloister and that the two constructions are close with regard to time.

Starting from the second half of the 16th century, with the new use of the complex as an orphanage, the cloister was also affected by the works of restoration and transformation. More precisely, larger arches on pillars were opened in place of the smaller ones, obtained by filling in the space between two couples of colonnettes, which in this way were preserved. It is likely that the barrel vaults covering the corridors, and the simple loggia on square pillars on the floor above, were constructed at the same time.

Other transformations later affected the perimeter areas, some of which are evident on the upper floor of the loggia from the coats-of-arms of Odoardo Farnese and Francesco Barberini, cardinal protectors of the Archconfraternity of the Orphans during the early 17th century. In the 17th or 18th century, the loggia on the west side was enclosed in order to create more rooms.

Between the late 18th and early 19th century some small rooms were created in the cloister corridors, which testify to their, by then, impoverished use. Of note among these was the 'painted room' situated in the north-east corner, which contained the iron door created in 1757, making it possible to reach the reliquary holding the head of St Sebastian, preserved in the altar named after him.

The present aspect of the cloister dates mainly to the radical restoration conducted between 1912 and 1916 by Antonio Muñoz, first inspector, later Superintendent of Ancient Monuments, whose objective was to restore as far as possible the 13th-century image of the cloister, but maintain the upper floor with the loggia and the barrel vaults that sustained it. Having demolished the small rooms that cluttered the corridors, Muñoz reinstated the small arches that had been destroyed as well as the missing decorations. A large part of the plaster wall surfaces was replaced and the present colouring was applied to all the surfaces, followed by a glaze whose purpose was to mitigate the contrast between the new and ancient sections.

Among the subsequent restoration works, we should mention that of the rooms on the west wing used for welcoming prayer groups (1981-82) and that of the library situated on the south side (2007). The garden was restored in 2005 on completion of the archaeological excavation, during which the ancient baptistry was discovered and then reburied for conservation purposes (see later).

4.5.2. The fountain

The fountain at the centre of the cloister, which contributes considerably to the charm of the site, was created by Antonio Muñoz in 1913. It consists of a square basin at the centre of which, standing on a base that imitates those of the 13th-century colonnettes, a section of fluted column supports an unusual element of mediaeval origin made out of two circular basins one above the other. The lower basin has a diameter of 1.61 m and the upper of 1.26, and was carved from a single block of Proconnesian marble that had evidently already been used. Muñoz took the basins and the section of column from another fountain situated in the cloister garden made from recovered pieces in 1627 by Cardinal Vidoni.

The lower basin features four protomes, through which the water flows, not easily identifiable because of the eroded marble. Between two of these there are

Fig. 88. *The cloister fountain: view from the east after its restoration in 2005 (sponsor: the Marra family).*

another two leonine protomes side by side. A hole for water to exit replaces the right eye of lion, which probably functions as an overflow.

The four protomes probably represented heads of real or fantastic marine animals, which are an iconographic theme linked to the presence of water, as the lion is too. In antiquity this, in fact, was considered as the one that safeguarded the purity of the waters and since then was often chosen as the mouth of a fountain (it must be noted, however, that in this case the lion protomes are not those through which the water principally passed).

The central element with two basins became incorrectly described as a *cantharus* or crater, a term that actually corresponds to a type of vase of a very different shape, even though it is often used in classical antiquity to describe decorative garden elements, fountains included. At least for the upper basin, however, the model was perhaps of classical age or Late Antiquity, or that of the marble *labra*, a type of water container also very widespread. The two-basin structure, instead, was frequently used for fountains in the Byzantine East as early as the 11th-12th century, whereas in the West it only became customary during the Late Middle Ages. This structure therefore comprises many components, from the classical and Palaeochristian heritage to influences of the Byzantine world, as well as new forms that developed in the eleventh and twelfth centuries and later became widespread.

Though for the moment being almost unique, the double basin of the cloister could easily be classified within the sphere of the revival and reinstatement of classical formulas that marked the beginning of the 12th century, and therefore could be compared with the works of Pascal II. It is not known where it was originally located: it may have been placed at the centre of one of the two courtyards that precede the basilica, with the pair of the lions probably positioned in the foreground.

Fig. 89, 90, 91. *Details of the protomes on the fountain after restoration in 2005.*

Fig. 92. *The cloister fountain: view from above after its restoration in 2005.*

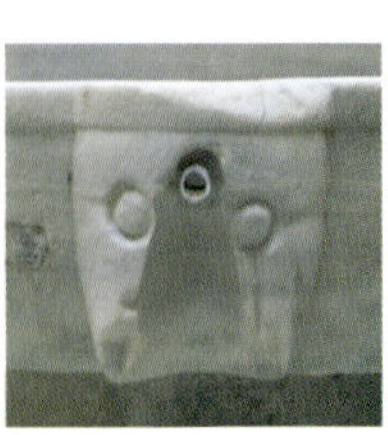

4.5.3. The antiquarium

Along the walls of the cloister Antonio Muñoz created an *antiquarium* consisting mainly of archaeological finds that had been inserted into the pavement of Pascal II's basilica. Of particular note on the east wall, we find a number of stone inscriptions originating from ancient Christian cemeteries: the most famous is the fragment of the epitaph poem written by Pope Damasus I (366-384) in honour of the martyrs Peter and Marcellinus, originally placed on their tomb in the catacomb of Via Labicana. Written in splendid so-called Philocalian script (named after Furius Dionysius Philocalus, the painter and calligrapher who invented it), it was discovered in the paving of a cistern situated in the cloister itself. The fragment, if not the entire stone inscription, may have been brought into the complex when Leo IV had the relics of the Four Saints transferred from the same catacomb. Other small fragments of the same inscription came to light in an ancient refuse storage room discovered in the tower of the quadriporticus.

Fig. 93. *Detail of the east wall of the cloister with the inscriptions displayed, among them that of the epitaph poem by Damasus I in honour of Saints Peter and Marcellinus (indicated by the arrow).*

Fig. 94. *Cloister. Early mediaeval altar-frontal (9th cent.?).*

Fig. 95. *Cloister. Game engraved on one of the slabs supporting the colonnettes.*

The south wall displays material mainly originating from the Early Middle Ages, among them fragments of plutei with their typical interwoven decorations.

On the west wall we find, in particular, fragments of liturgical fittings and Cosmati altars belonging to the late mediaeval phases of the basilica, remains of Roman cornices, and two front panels from classical sarcophagi that were reused upside down as altar mensas. It is also worth noting that the three walls already mentioned contain round-arched niches, typical of mediaeval buildings, which have a roof tile inserted at the back, and were often used for placing lamps inside.

Lastly, on the north wall where the entrance is, we find a collection of typical seals stamped on Roman bricks (in the north-west corner), a 15th-century sepulchral stone and two splendid fragments of classical marble entablature.

4.5.4. The chapel of St Barbara

The chapel, whose entrance is in the east wing of the cloister, formed part of the basilica of Leo IV and, together with its symmetrical counterpart St Nicholas (not open to the public), is one of the very few surviving early mediaeval oratories in Rome. The dedication to Santa Barbara was surmised by Antonio Muñoz, who recognized some episodes of her life in the 13th-century frescoes that cover it, and as a consequence identified it as the oratory dedicated to her existing within the basilica and cited in the *Liber Pontificalis.*

It has a trapezoidal almost square plan, whose irregularity is due to the fact that it was decided to site both oratories on the medial axis of the basilica, a position that, however, was to interfere with the external wall of the baptistry. It is covered by a cross vault, whose four finely carved marble corbels, one in each corner, are more decorative than functional. Probably below them there would have been columns that contributed to the sumptuousness of the architecture. The

Fig. 96. *Chapel of St Barbara (9th cent.). Exterior.*

Fig. 97. *Chapel of St Barbara (9th cent.). Interior restored by Antonio Muñoz in 1913-1914.*

Fig. 98. *Chapel of St Barbara. Detail of the face carved in place of a rosette on the south-east corbel.*

corbels represent the most important feature of the chapel: they are original Roman fragments partially reworked in the 9th century, as the small human face in place of a flower on the corbel in the south-west corner testifies. On the north side of the chapel, the large rectangular door was the original entrance to the Leonine basilica. At the centre of each of the other three sides, recessed apses are surmounted by rectangular windows with marble lattice-work. Only the west lattice moulding, obtained from a pluteus perhaps of the 8th-9th century, is original. The apse on the west side is pierced by the present door leading from the cloister.

At the time of Leo IV, the walls, with their irregular brick courses typical of 9th-century buildings in Rome, would be entirely covered with frescoes, of which only the fragments of two saints remain in the apse on the south side. The exterior wall of the chapel was also frescoed, as the fragment with a decorative motif above the door, just visible from the cloister, testifies. Again on the exterior, the walls and apses were capped by a cornice embellished with marble corbels with plant-like decorations typical of the 9th century. After being incorporated into the Benedictine monastery, the chapel was transformed: the recessed apses to the south and west were demolished and the door to the cloister was inserted: in so doing, the axis of the chapel was rotated by 90°. In the late 13th century it was also redecorated, part of which still exists today: in the remaining apse, which had become the fulcrum of the chapel, the figure of the Virgin enthroned with Child and two saints were frescoed; at the height of the corbels a frieze was painted with geometrical motifs that recall those on the panels of the Cosmati mosaic in the cloister; above, episodes of the life of the saints were painted with the symbols of the Evangelists on the vault. As regards the latter, their similarity to those of the vault of *Sancta Sanctorum*, at the time of Nicholas III (1277-1280) is evident.

We owe the present aspect of the chapel to Antonio Muñoz who, among other things, had the south and west apses reconstructed (which, in fact, have different masonry) and hung the plaster moulds on the walls of the plutei that we find reused the other way round in the parapets of the galleries inside the basilica.

4.5.5. The baptistry

Its remains, almost razed to the ground, were discovered in the south-east sector of the cloister, covered by a thick layer of debris containing a lot of carbonized materials dating to the 11th-12th century. This layer can be linked to the works resulting from the Norman fire of 1084, which brought about an overall increase in height of ground level and the construction of a first cloister on a square plan in place of the baptistry.

As regards the baptistry, only a quarter of which was brought to light, it is possible to surmise that it was circular in shape with a diameter of twelve metres; the perimeter wall was in brick with marble cladding; a door opened to the north, di-

Fig. 99. *Detail of the baptismal font discovered during the archaeological excavation of the cloister conducted in 2002-2004 (sponsors: Antigua Foundation and Robert Wilson).*

rectly facing the place of worship, at the time situated in the hall of the *domus*. The ambulatory was about three metres wide and remains of two paved floors were discovered there, the original one made with small slabs of polychrome marble; the later, perhaps dating to the 9th century made with large slabs of recovered marble.

The baptismal font was at the centre of the area, also on a circular plan of at least six metres in diameter, built with masonry cladded with white marble and Cipolin slabs; three non-continuous steps led down to it. Eight blocks of travertine were embedded in the parapet, which was animated by at least one counter curve. These blocks must have sustained the same number of columns all linked to one another by an architrave, on which curtains would hang to conceal the ceremony in progress and which would also support a cover, either of the font alone or of the central part of the room, as in the Lateran Baptistry. The large number of *tubuli* (small terracotta tubes pointed at one end, used to make concentric rings, one inserted into the other, with which lightweight vaults were constructed) discovered in the excavated debris together with numerous glass tesserae lead us to believe that the baptistry was at one time covered with mosaic.

As far as its date is concerned, the limited data still under study seems to place it around the 5th century AD.

4.6. The rooms of the Cardinal's Palace

4.6.1. The *Calendar* room

The almost square room covered by a circa 17th-century wood ceiling, is the present anteroom of the Augustine Nuns' parlour, but was itself used as a parlour until not long ago, as indicated by the foundling wheel for the exchange of objects and the partially filled-in openings with the grate that permitted the nuns to communicate.

The room was obtained in the 13th century from within the right aisle of the Leonine basilica, by filling in the arcade and creating two new separating walls to

Fig. 100. *The* Calendar *room, today the entrance hall of the monastery of the Augustinian Nuns.*

Fig. 101. *Detail of the* Calendar *with the months of* January *and* February.

the east and west. It was originally illuminated by narrow single windows (two are visible from the courtyard, two from the parlour), which were filled in to create the cycle of frescoes depicting a calendar, from which the name of the room derives. This cycle is the first of the three that the visitor encounters, presumably commissioned in the mid-13th century by Cardinal Stefano Conti, and the one that is unfortunately less preserved. Already with many parts of the frescoes missing, it was whitewashed over in 1632 and brought back to light by Antonio Muñoz in 1913. It was restored in 1968 and again in 2008.

The cycle was divided into at least three registers. At the top, twelve figures (only two remain, headless, on the south wall) personified the months of the year and held the unfolded scrolls of parchment in their hands upon which the calendar was transcribed. The figures were inserted into the painted arches, which from their proportions must have been three-foiled, supported by pillars with candelabra motifs.

Four months are depicted on each wall, with the exception of the east wall that reveals no evidence of past decoration, from where a door leads into the chapel of St Sylvester. The calendar commences on the south wall from the left with the month of January and continues in a clockwise direction. The parchments are divided into four columns: in the first, we find the golden number (a number from 1 to 19 used for the calculation of the full moons); in the second, the dominical letter - a letter of the alphabet from A to G that corresponded to the day of the week (these first two columns enabled the calculation of the moveable feast of Easter); in the third, the day according to the ancient Roman use is indicated and, finally, in the last column the name of the saint who is venerated on that day or the recurrence of a particular feast. The script is typically Gothic with red and black letters, and the variation in the characters indicates that several artists were involved. Under the months, another band divided into panels depicted the human activities of each month; under December (east corner of north wall) it was still possible to discern the figure of a farmer slaughtering a pig until the 1970s. Lastly, the lower register was painted with imitation drapery, of which a small section still survives on the north wall.

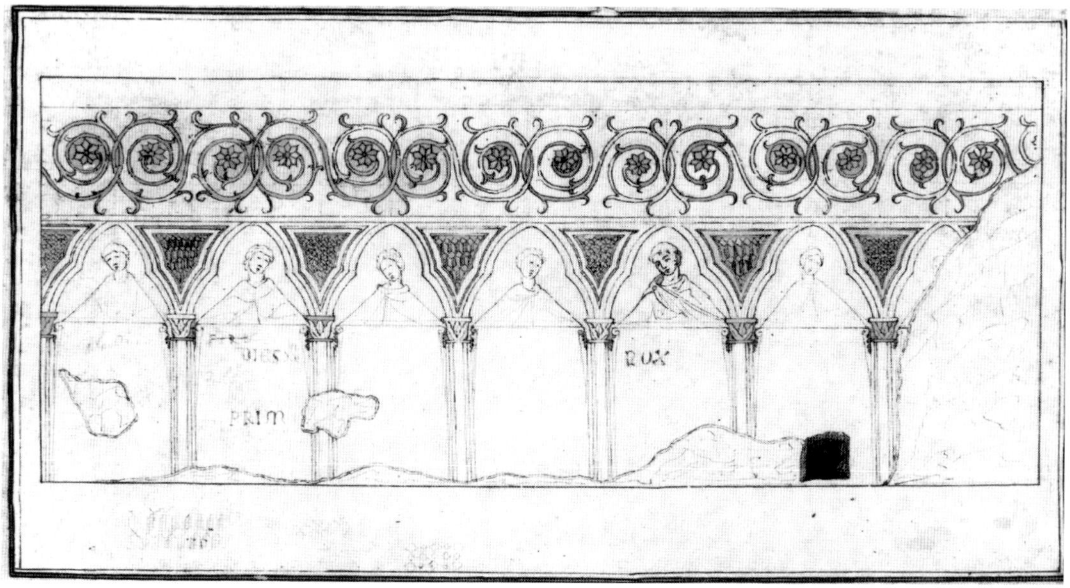

Fig. 102. *The lost* Calendar *of the Monastery of the Tre Fontane in Rome in a drawing by J.-B.-L.-G. Seroux d'Agincourt (Biblioteca Apostolica Vaticana,* Vat. Lat. *9847,* fol. *18*r*).*

The original door, as a small surviving section of its painted edging indicates, was situated on the south wall in place of the window that overlooks the courtyard, under the months of March and April, whose scrolls of parchment are, in fact, shorter. The calendar was created after 1235, the year Elizabeth of Hungary - whose feast is recorded - was canonized, and is assumed to be earlier than 1246 due to the absence of Edmund of Canterbury, canonized in that year and usually present in late 13th-century calendars. In any case, some other important saints canonized in the years 1253-54 are also missing. The following painted inscription was inserted on 24 April: O[BIIT] R[ICHARDUS] COMES PAT[ER] S[TEPHANI] C[ARDINALIS], which records the death of Riccardo, father of Stefano Conti, in 1226.

From these dates, it is possible to conclude that Stefano Conti commissioned the calendar, whose execution took place after 1235 and before his death in 1254, probably around 1246, or just before the consecration of the adjoining chapel in 1247. This means that the decoration of the two rooms formed part of a single decorative plan desired by the cardinal, in which the hall above must also have been included. In fact, the calendar has many elements in common with or, in some instances, identical to the decoration in the hall above, such as the candelabra motifs that divide the arches or the calligraphy of certain letters.

The peculiarity of this cycle is precisely the presence of written text, which was common in illuminated manuscripts, but not in painting, where the representation of the months usually consisted in illustrating the tasks specific to each one of them. The lost calendar of the Tre Fontane Monastery in Rome, dating perhaps to a few decades later, also depicted a written text.

The use of the calendar is strictly linked to the presence of the adjoining chapel and contains indications of events that were important to the cardinal, such as the death of his father. As with the other cycles desired by Stefano Conti, it also carries specific political import, in that the feast days of the early popes take priority in it, an evident reference to the purity of the Church and its origins.

4.6.2. The chapel of St Sylvester

From the *Calendar* room we enter the chapel of St Sylvester, situated on the ground floor of the Great Tower, built at the request of Cardinal Stefano Conti, who had it consecrated in 1247.

From the very beginning, it was composed of two parts separated by a round arch: a small nave covered by a barrel vault and illuminated by a single window on the south side; a rectangular presbytery three steps higher up and positioned as is customary to the east, originally covered by a cross vault and illuminated by two narrow single windows surmounted by an oculus on the back wall and by another oculus on the right wall, the latter today filled in but visible from the first courtyard. The openings are all splayed in a downward direction to provide more light.

The plan has some irregularities in that the chapel was constructed in an area lying between the eastern end of the right aisle of the Leonine basilica and the north-west corner of the quadriporticus that preceded it, structures that were partially incorporated into the new ones. Evidently, the builders wanted to reutilize the arch, which in the 9th century linked the north and west wings of the quadriporticus, as the entrance arch to the presbytery, despite the fact that this would create an asymmetrical solution.

Of the frescoes that originally covered the entire chapel, the cycle narrating the *Episodes from the Life of Pope Sylvester* (314-335) are preserved in the nave: among them, the famous Donation with which Constantine supposedly ceded Rome, the Italian provinces and the Western regions to the pope, an act on which the temporal power of the Church and the supremacy of the pope over the emperor were founded, and the reason why the legend of Sylvester had assumed such political importance in the Middle Ages.

The narration begins on the back of the entrance façade to the left. The first panel depicts the emperor Constantine, struck by leprosy, reassuring a group of women with their offspring. According to the priests of the Temple of Jupiter on the Capitol, he would be cured from the terrible disease by taking a bath in children's blood, but moved to pity he renounced the idea. In the second episode, the ailing emperor is visited in a dream by the apostles Peter and Paul, who advise him to seek out Pope Sylvester; in the third panel, three messengers on horseback head towards Mount Soracte where the pope had taken refuge to escape persecution.

Fig. 103. *Chapel of St Sylvester. Plan of the existing state with the structures of the basilica of Leo IV outlined in green; those of the palace of Stefano Conti in blue; and the 16th and 17th-century transformations in yellow.*

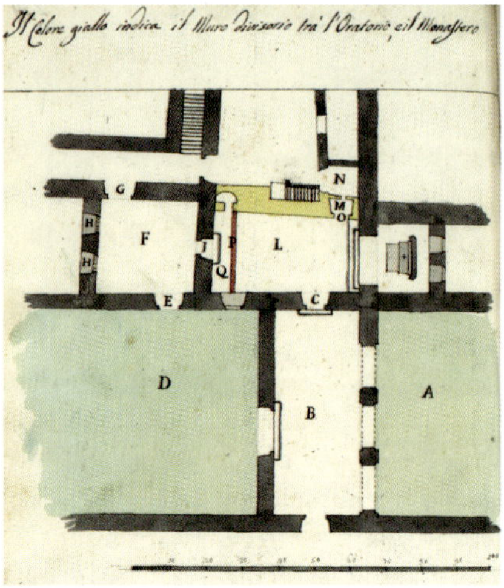

Fig. 104. *Chapel of St Sylvester. Plan from 1794 with the position of the partition to be constructed (Archivio di Stato di Roma,* Trenta Notai Capitolini, Simonetti Franciscus Xaverius, ufficio 29, vol. 477, fol. 139v).

Fig. 105. *Chapel of St Sylvester. View towards the presbytery.*

Above these, the lunette of the vault depicts Christ enthroned as Judge, flanked on his right by the Virgin and on his left by St John the Baptist, and by two angels and the twelve Apostles equitably divided on each side. Christ displays his wounds with the cross to the left and the symbols of the Passion to the right: the lance, crown of thorns, nails and sponge. The depiction of the Last Judgement, which was fairly common on the back of entrance façades, is based on the Apocalypse of St John. The angel on the left, in fact, holds a scroll which depicts a black sun, a moon and stars: this is a reference to the opening of the sixth seal «And I saw, when he had opened the sixth seal, and behold there was a great earthquake, and the sun became black as sackcloth of hair: and the whole moon became as blood [...] And the heaven departed as a book folded up» (*Apoc.* 6: 12-14).

The story continues on the left wall: in the first panel, the heavenly messengers climb Mount Soracte to reach the papal retreat; in the second, Pope Sylvester

Fig. 106. *Chapel of St Sylvester. Back of the entrance façade with the* Last Judgement *and three episodes from the* Lives of Sylvester and Constantine *(second quarter of 13th cent.).*

on returning to Rome shows Constantine the true images of Peter and Paul, so that he can identify the figures that appeared to him in his dream; in the third, the emperor, stripped of his imperial robes, is baptized by immersion by Sylvester. In the fourth, Constantine restored to health wearing his imperial robes, leaves a gate leading a white horse, genuflects and offers the tiara to the pope seated on the throne, while another acolyte offers the pope an *umbraculum*, a parasol with red and yellow stripes; the emperor does not have the crown, which is held by a figure standing above the entrance gate of a palace identified as the Capitol by the barely legible inscription below the panel: the pope, in fact, supposedly refused the crown offered him by the emperor. In the final episode, Sylvester, with the tiara on his head, rides a white steed accompanied by Constantine, this time with his crown, but on foot holding the bridle in an act of homage and pointing to a

Fig. 107. *Chapel of St Sylvester, north side with episodes of the* Baptism of Constantine, *the* Donation, *and the* Officium stratoris *(second quarter of 13th cent.).*

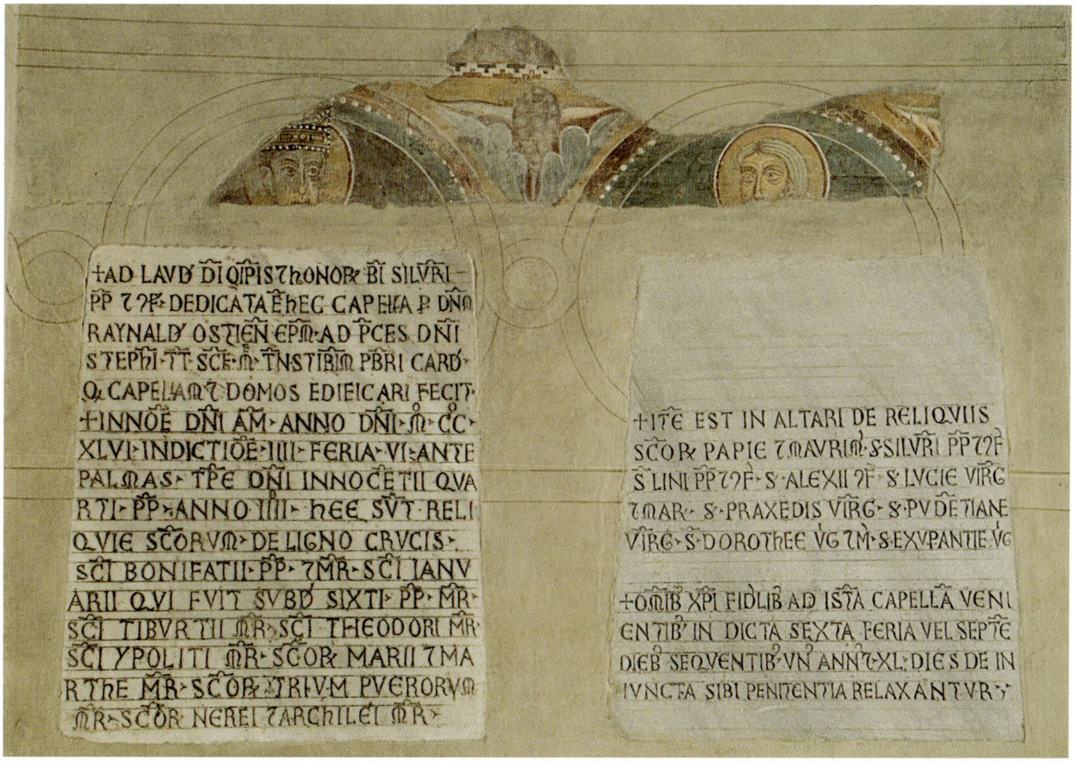

Fig. 108. *Chapel of St Sylvester, south side. Inscription of the consecration of 1247, which cuts off the medallions of two figures from the Old Testament: (left tablet) †AD LAUD[EM] D[E]I O[MN]IP[OTENT]IS ET HONOR[EM] B[EAT]I SILV[EST]RI/P[A]P[E] ET CON[FESSOR]IS. DEDICATA E[ST] HEC CAPELLA P[ER] D[OMI]N[U]M/RAYNALD[UM] OSTIEN[SEM] EP[ISCOPU]M AD P[RE]CES D[OMI]NI/STEPH[AN]I T[I]T[ULI] S[AN]C[T]E M[ARI]E T[RA]NSTIB[ER]IM P[RES]B[YTE]RI CARD[INALIS]/Q[UI] CAPELLAM ET DOMOS EDIFICARI FECIT./†IN NO[MIN]E D[OMI]NI AM[EN]. ANNO D[OMI]NI M CC/XLVI INDICTIO[N]E IIII FERIA VI ANTE/PALMAS. T[EM]P[OR]E D[OMI]NI INNOCE[N]TII QUA/RTI P[AP]E ANNO IIII. HEE SU[N]T RELI/QUIE S[AN]C[T]ORUM. DE LIGNO CRUCIS/S[AN]C[T]I BONIFATII P[A]P[E] ET M[ARTI]R[YS] S[AN]C[T]I IANU/ARII QUI FUIT SUBD[IACONUS] SIXTI P[A]P[E] M[ARTI]R[YS]/S[AN]C[T]I TIBURTII M[ARTY]R[IS] S[AN]C[T]I THEODORI M[ARTY]R[IS]/S[AN]C[T]I YPOLITI M[ARTY]R[IS] S[AN]C[T]ORUM MARII ET MA/RTHE M[ARTY]R[UM] S[AN]C[T]ORUM TRIUM PUERORUM/M[ARTY]R[UM] S[AN]C[T]ORUM NEREI ET ARCHILEI M[ARTY]R[UM]; (right tablet) †ITE[M] EST IN ALTARI DE RELIQUIIS/S[AN]C[T]ORUM PAPIE ET MAURI M[ARTYRUM] S[ANCTI] SILV[EST]RI P[A]P[E] ET CONF[ESSORIS]/S[ANCTI] LINI P[A]P[E] ET CONF[ESSORIS] S[ANCTI] ALEXII CONF[ESSORIS] S[ANCTE] LUCIE VIRG[INIS]/ET MAR[TYRIS] S[ANCTE] PRAXEDIS VIRG[INIS] S[ANCTE] PUDE[N]TIANE/VIRG[INIS] S[ANCTE] DOROTHEE VI[R]G[INIS] ET M[ARTYRIS] S[ANCTE] EXUP[ER]ANTIE VI[R]G[INIS]/†OM[N]IB[US] CHR[IST]I FID[E]LIB[US] AD ISTA[M] CAPELLA[M] VENI/ENTIB[US] IN DICTA SEXTA FERIA VEL SEPTE[M]/DIEB[US] SEQUENTIB[US] UN[US] ANN[US] ET XL DIES DE IN/IUNCTA SIBI PENITENTIA RELAXANTUR (This chapel was dedicated to Almighty God and to honour the blessed pope and confessor Sylvester by Rainaldus, bishop of Ostia, who embraced the prayers of Stefano, cardinal priest of S. Maria in Trastevere, who saw to the construction of the chapel and* domus. *In the name of God, Amen. The year of Our Lord 1246, indiction IV, on the Friday before Palm Sunday, in the fourth year of the pontificate of Innocent IV. These are the relics of the saints: some wood from the Cross, of St Boniface pope and martyr, of St Januarius who was subdeacon, of Sixtus pope and martyr, of St Tiburtius martyr, of St Theodore martyr, of St Hippolytus martyr, of Saints Marius and Martha martyrs, of the Three Virgin Martyr Saints, of Saints Nereus and Achilleus martyrs. Similarly in the altar there are the relics of Saints Papia and Maurus martyrs, of St Sylvester pope and confessor, of St Linus pope and confessor, of St Alexius confessor, of St Lucy virgin martyr, of St Praxedes virgin martyr, of St Potentiana virgin, of St Dorothy virgin martyr, of St Esuperantia virgin. To all the faithful who come to this chapel on the aforesaid Friday or within the next seven days an indulgence of a year and forty days is granted).*

Fig. 109. *Chapel of St Sylvester, south side.* Sylvester overcomes the rabbi Zambri; Invention of the True Cross *(second quarter of 13th cent.). Above, the listening funnels inserted into the frieze; below left, the inscription of the consecration of 1247.*

Fig. 110. *Chapel of St Sylvester, south side. Detail of listening funnel.*

palace, perhaps that of the Lateran; in front of him, two dignitaries bear the cross and sword, symbols of the two powers. It is the most ancient depiction of the *officium stratoris,* an act that signified vassalic submission and that, in this case, clearly indicates the emperor's role of subservience to the pope.

The episodes on the right wall refer solely to the life of Sylvester. In the first on the left, the pope (no longer visible) upholds the supremacy of the Christian over the Jewish faith in court in the presence of the rabbi Zambri and resuscitates the wild bull that the latter had struck dead only with his voice; two judges preside at the centre, while to the right in the background we observe the empress Helen, mother of Constantine, distinguishable by her crown, who was on the side of Zambri. The second represents the *Invention of the True Cross,* an episode that was inserted into some ancient versions of the legend of Sylvester: Helen, by then converted to Christianity and surrounded by her attendants, verifies which of the three crosses discovered on Golgotha was that of Christ: only the True Cross would be able to raise a man (the man laid out with greenish skin) from the dead. The final episode, much of which has disappeared, depicts Sylvester perhaps in the act of transferring the Cross to Rome. In the red band that runs below the episodes there are explanatory inscriptions, most of them missing, in which it is still possible to read the names *Constantinus* and *Silvester.* The episodes are framed by decorative borders; the upper one consists of plant volutes, into which two shell-shaped marble funnels were inserted on the south side. These are connected to two conduits made of terracotta tubes, which terminate in the Gothic Hall above, where similar funnels were placed about 1.60 m above floor level. They allowed the sacred liturgy in the chapel to be heard from the floor above.

The lower band contained twenty-seven medallions, many of them now lost or with many lacunae, portraying busts of the prophets and other Old Testament figures, who hold scrolls containing lines of verse. The texts as well as the names inscribed to the side of the figures have almost all completely disappeared, but

Fig. 111. *Chapel of St Sylvester, west side. The* Dream of Constantine *(second quarter of 13th cent.).*

Fig. 112. *Chapel of St Sylvester, north side. The* Donation of Constantine *(second quarter of 13th cent.).*

Fig. 113. *Chapel of St Sylvester. The north side of the presbytery (last quarter of 16th cent.): on the wall, the* Martyrdom of the four Roman soldiers *attributed to Raffaellino da Reggio.*

have been passed down via a copy made in 1637 by Antonio Eclisse, artist appointed by Cardinal Francesco Barberini to reproduce paintings and sculptures of Christian Rome. The overall significance is that of the prefiguration of future events in the Old Testament, which the figures express through their words.

No traces of decoration remain on the lower walls of the nave, but it is probable that there were frescoes of imitation drapery, as in the adjoining *Calendar* room. The vault, which was also full of lacunae and reintegrated in 1913, is decorated with eight-point green and red stars on a whitish ground, to imitate the vault of heaven. At the centre, five majolica cups have surprisingly been inserted into the vault arranged in the form of a cross. While the use of ceramics was customary for exterior surfaces, particularly of bell towers, this example in an interior appears to be unique.

Under the episode of the *Resurrection of the bull* we find the inscriptions that record the construction and consecration of the chapel and list the relics of the altar. They consist of two tablets originally located in the lower jambs of the two single apsidal windows, which, in fact, have their trapezoidal shape and dimensions, and were moved to their present position after circa 1670. The presbytery appears today in the guise conferred upon it towards the end of the 16th century by the University of Marble Workers and it is impossible to reconstruct its original decoration. The modern Crucifixion painted on the back wall may have replaced a similar subject, as we find, for example, in the church of S. Maria ad Cryptas at Fossa in Abruzzo, of a not much later date. Although entirely hypothetical, there may have been episodes of the life of the Virgin on the walls, a reason that may have induced their depiction on the external walls of the portico (see earlier) in 1588, and therefore shortly after the destruction of the original frescoes. The original 13th-century decoration was completed by a Cosmati mosaic pavement, of which the area of the presbytery and the central area of the nave remain intact, featuring a series of *rotae*.

The themes depicted in the nave were intended for a cultured public - such as that comprising the members of the curia - that had been taught how to interpret the Holy Scriptures from a prefigurational standpoint, which testifies to the essentially 'private' use of the chapel. In the past, these frescoes were negatively appraised: they supposedly represented the fading embers of Byzantine tendencies in Rome at the moment in which, instead, a new cultural trend of a Gothic matrix was emerging. This appraisal must today be completely reassessed in the light of the discovery of the frescoes of the Gothic Hall (see later).

Fig. 114. *Chapel of St Sylvester. Detail from the fresco on the right wall of the presbytery, depicting* Nicodemus retrieving the boxes with the remains of the five stonemasons from the sea *(photo: L. Barelli).*

As regards the presbytery, shortly after the acquisition of the chapel by the Marble Workers, its dimensions were reduced by adding two masonry linings so as to obtain a more traditional shape, in which the width would be less than that of the nave. The cross vault was replaced by a domical vault and the wall surfaces were completely redecorated.The left wall depicts the martyrdom of the four soldiers (*cornicularii)* close to the statue of Asclepius (in the background in miniature, the scene of the bodies being offered to the dogs); on the right wall, instead, the five stonemasons are enclosed in lead boxes close to the statue of the Sun-God (in the background, Nicodemus retrieves the boxes from the sea); the back wall has the *Annunciation* at the top and below a *Crucifixion* inside a stucco frame, around which the wall is decorated with grotesches. The images of Constantine and Sylvester are portrayed on the two pillars of the arch. The vault is divided into compartments in which the four *cornicularii* are represented (with, however, stonemasons' tools in their hands!) with the four Evangelists and four angels that hold up a clipeus bearing the image of the Blessing Redeemer.

These frescoes, certainly completed before 1588, when they were cited by the historian Pompeo Ugonio, are generally attributed to the Roman production of Raffaellino Motta da Reggio, who worked in Rome under Gregory XIII (1572-1585). The death of the painter in 1578 supposedly happened before the completion of the frescoes, a fact that would explain the poor execution on the lower section of the right wall, done by an assistant. As regards the vault and *Annunciation,* the name of the Florentine painter Giovanni Battista Vanni, active in Rome between 1624 and 1632, has also been put forward.

In 1727, the chapel was restored by the mediocre painter Cristoforo Cagnardi, who covered the vault of the nave and the decorative 13th-century borders above and below the St Sylvester episodes with a decoration painted with geomet-

Fig. 115. *Chapel of St Sylvester. The south side of the presbytery (last quarter of 16th cent.): on the arch,* Constantine*; on the wall,* Martyrdom of the five stonemasons *attributed to Raffaellino da Reggio.*

rical partitions containing palms and crowns alluding to the martyrdom, at the centre of which he attached a canvas with four angels holding crowns. It is interesting to note how on this occasion the *Episodes from the Life of Sylvester* and *Constantine*, by then completely out of fashion, were left visible, perhaps because of their political and historical significance, which must have still been very evident. To conclude this project, the altar was rebuilt and consecrated on 27 June 1728 by Benedict XIII, as the inscription carved on the altar itself records.

The lateral strips of paving in the nave were replaced with black and white marble stone elements perhaps leftovers from the pavement remade by Borromi-

Fig. 116. *Chapel of St Sylvester, presbytery. The frescoed vault (last quarter of 16th cent.?).*

ni at San Giovanni in Laterano for the 1650 Jubilee. To the left, an inscription in the pavement indicates the burial site of members of the Annone family, stonemasons originating from Como, starting with Matteo (d. 1576), and on the wall another stone inscription records the bequest of the son of these, Giovanni Pietro, to celebrate a mass on the day of his own death every year.

The mixed attendance of nuns and university members in the chapel began to create discord. Following a dispute resolved in 1794 and recorded on an inscription originally placed at the centre of the south side, the chapel was divided into two by a masonry partition, of which the smaller west part was reserved for the priest to hear the nuns' confession via a small door situated in the north-west corner.

New interest in the chapel was shown at the beginning of the 20th century when the art historian Federico Hermanin had the two episodes on either side of the *Invention of the Cross* uncovered. These had, in fact, been whitewashed over, perhaps because of their many lacunae, after 1637 when Eclisse still reproduces them, and probably in 1686 when some works involving painting were recorded. A comprehensive restoration work, however, was only carried out by Antonio Muñoz in 1913, who removed the partition (whose carved outline is still visible in the pavement close to the entrance), uncovered the hidden areas of frescoes, reintegrating their lacunae with coloured grounds, but without details, moved the stone inscription recording the dispute between the nuns and marble workers below the other inscriptions, and reinstated the original access to the *Calendar* room, which was, however, only opened at a later date. This intervention was followed by many others, such as that of Arnolfo Crucianelli in 1950, who replaced the coloured reintegrated areas with incised outlines on a neutral ground, until the most recent one in the nave in 2006.

Fig. 117. *Gothic hall. Detail of various birds depicted on the cornice that divides the registers.*

4.6.3. The Gothic Hall

The so-called Gothic Hall (book visit at entrance in first courtyard) is situated on the first floor of the Great Tower and was the most prestigious room of the palace constructed by Stefano Conti, where receptions and banquets were held, and where justice was administered (Conti, in fact, like the other cardinals, acted as magistrate of the tribunal of the Curia).

The hall owes its importance to the architectonic forms in the Gothic style, which are exceptional for the city of Rome, and to the extraordinary pictorial cycle that covers its walls. The latter, which was covered by successive layers of paint, was restored by the State Superintendences over a ten-year period. Its discovery (1995) led to the necessity for a complete re-evaluation of the history of 13th-century painting in Rome. On the one hand, it testifies to a substantial and, for many aspects, unexpected introduction of Gothic culture within the Roman domain, which finds a parallel in that identifiable in the architecture of the hall; on the other, it demonstrates a conscious and highly cultured revival of the classical tradition.

The room that houses the cycle is a grandiose space of an almost rectangular

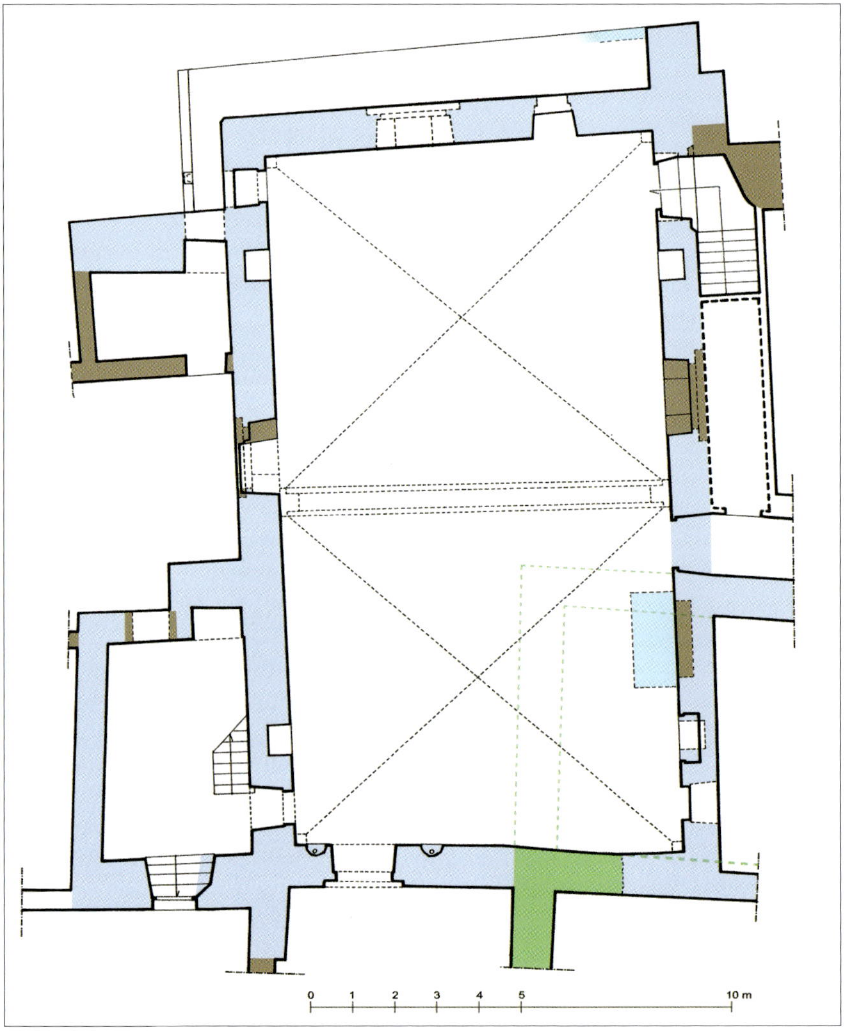

Fig. 118. *Gothic hall. Plan at the level of the windows with seats: (in green, the wall of the Leonine nave; in blue, the walls of the first phase of the Great Tower; in light blue, the demolished fireplace and parapet; and in brown, the 13th-century transformations).*

plan of about 9 x 17.5 m, 11.5 m in height, divided by a transversal arch of peperino stone ashlars into two bays covered by pointed cross vaults without ribs, resting upon stone corbels. The walls are made with *tufelli*, except for a number of repair works and a section of the south wall in brick, which is very uneven. This section of wall is none other than the right corner wall of the nave of the Leonine

Fig. 119. *Gothic hall. View to the south.*

Fig. 120. *Gothic hall. The window with seats on the west side.*

Fig. 121. *Gothic hall. Detail of a frescoed basket on the north side.*

Fig. 122. *Gothic hall. Detail of imprint from the reed matting on the vault.*

Fig. 123. *Gothic hall. West wall of south bay.*

basilica incorporated into the construction. The vaults are of particular interest from a technical standpoint, which like those of the Roman era, are made of concrete. The wood framework needed to construct them was covered with woven reeds, the imprints of which remain on the intradoses.

As with similar contemporary buildings, small rooms for private use were connected to the hall. On the north side, there was also an external balcony that perhaps led to the latrines. It is interesting to note that the doors and windows of the hall are positioned in an asymmetrical manner precisely because of the presence of these adjoining rooms.

The hall was connected to these rooms by six doors - two of which were larger - that all have a rectangular shape with a brick lintel on either the inner or outer wall of the hall, and smaller frames with pointed arches on their interior or exterior counterpart. The unusualness of these doors is that their frames are generally facing outwards or towards wider and therefore colder rooms, in order to reduce heat loss. The doorframes, which on the part facing inwards, were also covered by pictorial decorations, were made of peperino stone ashlars with the exception of those of the large door on the south wall that has alternating blocks of peperino and white marble, giving it more prominence. This door, however, was probably not the most important of the hall: the one situated in the north-west corner, today mostly concealed by subsequent structures is not only the widest but also the only one that has carved leaves on the impost of the arch. This leads us to suppose that the main access to the hall was from the existing staircase on the west side, originally positioned externally in a courtyard to which access was gained from the *Calendar* room. It is not by chance that the external oculus above the staircase is the only one in peperino.

Fig. 124. *Gothic hall. South wall of south bay.*

Today the hall is illuminated by three large windows of modern manufacture, but previously the light was filtered from numerous openings (partially reopened in recent restoration works) of varying shapes and sizes according to their height from the pavement: high up, oculi with splayed brickwork to direct the light downwards; rectangular windows in the middle section, similarly splayed with external frames made of alternating marble and peperino ashlars; lastly, in the lower

Fig. 125. *Gothic hall. East wall of south bay.*

part of the walls there were large windows, probably with two lights, again rectangular but with interior masonry seats, typical of residential architecture of the time.

Again in its original state, a large fireplace on the west wall of the south wing completed the decor of the hall, evident from the corbels supporting the chimney-hood, cut back to the level of the masonry wall, the bricked-up chimney breast and the vent hole, today sealed off but visible in the vault.

The hall was modified in a period relatively close to when it was decorated: the fireplace was removed, and the east and west windows with seats, as well as those in the middle section to the south and west and the oculus on the west wall of the north bay, were filled in, while the central window to the east was enlarged cutting into the fresco. These transformations were due to the construction, always in the 13th century, of new adjacent rooms, among them the Gothic gallery to the south and a room adjoining the west wall of the north bay, which later collapsed but of which external traces of the roof and ogival windows that overlooked Via dei Ss. Quattro still remain.

The frescoes originally covered the entire wall surface of the hall, but of these almost exclusively the parts comprising the lunettes of the vaults remain. The lower section of the walls must have been mainly decorated with imitation marble inlays or drapery, as was the custom at that time. Some fragments of painting remain on the south side, in particular in the left corner where a pillar is painted and in the lunette above the door where a lion is depicted attacking a deer. Again on the south wall two holes on either side of the door, where two marble funnels had been fitted, indicate the arrival point of the pipes from the chapel of St Sylvester below, which enabled one to hear the liturgy in progress. In the central section of the same wall, two fragments of a 17th-century decoration were left during restoration.

Four small niches were positioned, one at each end of the long walls, and frescoes that decorated the south-east and north-west ones still remain: a flower between two birds and a scene of murder (perhaps *Cain killing Abel*) respectively.

In the lunettes the decoration of the two bays, though different, is divided up in a similar way by decorative elements, among them the cornice that divides the two surviving registers stands out, with classical corbels studded with precious stones, on which birds of different species perch. At the impost of both the vaults above the classical capitals, telamones (male figures posed as if supporting an architectonic element) give the impression they are bearing the weight of the overlying covering. The figurative areas should be read in a precise order: first the south bay, then the north; first the lower register, then gradually the higher ones culminating at the apex of the vault; within each individual register, one proceeds in an anticlockwise direction in the south bay and a clockwise direction in the north bay, both of them starting from the west joint of the dividing arch. There is also a less spontaneous second order of reading, from below going upwards for every single wall of each bay.

Description of the subjects of the south bay

In the lower register, below curved arches consisting of sinuous dolphins with their tails intertwined (a motif of classical origin), the *Months of the Year* are represented: each one comprises the personification of the month and the depiction of the rural activities associated with it. The personification of *January* is of particular note, an old man with the aspect of the Roman God Janus portrayed here with three faces, or that of *March*, a youth from whose foot a woman removes a thorn. The decorative motifs above and below depict youthful cherubic figures, some of them winged, dressed only in cloaks.

In the upper register we find the personifications of the liberal arts starting with *Grammar*, followed by *Geometry*, *Music*, *Mathematics* and *Astronomy*: these are represented by maidens that dance close to enthroned figures who have exercised these arts in an exemplary manner, and whose names have since disappeared.

Fig. 126. *Gothic hall. The month of* March.

Fig. 127. *Gothic hall. The month of* May.

Fig. 128. *Gothic hall. The month of* September.

Fig. 129. *Gothic hall. Detail of* Music.

Above the telamones at the impost of the vault we find the *Seasons*, represented by four men of different ages, positioned next to their respective months and encircled by the *Winds*, portrayed as winged faces that blow. *Astronomy* introduces the subjects depicted on the central part of the vault, almost entirely lost. The remains of three circular registers are present: the first contained a *Marine landscape* (indicating the confines of the world); the second, the *Signs of the Zodiac* of which *Aquarius* with fragments of *Pisces* and *Capricorn* on either side and part of *Taurus* and *Scorpio* remain; lastly, the third represented the constellations of which only part of *Andromeda* has survived. As a result of analogies with similar iconographic themes, we can suppose that the centre of the vault may have depicted the personification of the *Year*.

In this bay we can note the substantial reintegration work carried out on the frescoes due to the removal of the fireplace, which affects the figures of *January*, *February*, the woman removing the thorn from the foot of *March* and in the upper register, the representation of *Grammar*. Evidently the frescoes originally covered the chimney-hood: *January* and the woman must have been depicted on the sides, while the month of *February* occupied the space at the front. The latter, in fact, which is today the only one restricted to a single figure positioned outside the curved arches, would in this way have had the same amount of space as the others. Also the anomalous composition of *Grammar*, where two figures appear enthroned and the space for the maiden who personifies the art is missing, must have been diversely arranged around the sides of the hood. Lastly, the corbelled frieze now poorly linked up where reintegration has taken place, would have been neatly positioned around the sides and front of the hood.

Description of the subjects of the north bay

In the lower register, again below the curved arches of dolphins, there are frescoes of the personifications of the *Virtues* and *Beatitudes*: women in military dress, capable consequently of resisting evil, who bear a figure from the Old or New Testament or a saint upon their shoulders, each of them distinguished in their field. At the same time they trample on two smaller figures that represent the opposing vice and a historical figure notorious for that vice: the series is interrupted at the centre of the wall by *King Solomon*, the epitome of Justice. A decorative motif with chaste female clothed figures runs above, which ideally counters the naked or semi-naked male figures on the opposite side.

In the upper register, the figures used to be arranged symmetrically: on the west side only *Mithras killing a bull* remains; to the north, two half-naked elderly figures with cornucopias and baskets of fruit and flowers (personifications of rivers or abundance) in their hands; to the east, the personifications of the *Sun* (Christ) on a horse-drawn chariot and the Moon (the Church) on a chariot drawn by oxen.

Of the decoration in the vault only the four telamones on capitals have survived, though with lacunae. The figures on the shoulders of the *Virtues* seem to be depicted in chronological order and possibly indicate the path of the Church up until the more recently canonized Sts Francis and Dominic. Only Peter does not respect this order, because he should have been depicted on the north wall next to Solomon, in a mirror position with respect to Paul and before Sts Lawrence and Augustine. His transfer to the east wall is perhaps justified by the vertical reading of the three walls: to the west, above the *Virtues* who support Old Testament figures is Mithras, the symbol of salvation and victory over the obscure forces of evil; to the north, above the *Virtues* who represent characteristics of a good government that follows the law of God, we find the abundance and fertility that derive from them; above, the history of the Church from St Peter to St Dominic, and lastly, we have the triumph of Christ and of the Church itself. The overall sense of the entire cycle would certainly have been better explained by the missing parts of the vault.

The frescoes of the hall together with those of the chapel of St Sylvester and the *Calendar* room form part of a single decoration project commissioned by Cardinal

Fig. 130. *Gothic hall.* Mithras killing a bull.

Fig. 131. *Gothic hall. North wall of north bay.*

Stefano Conti and presumably carried out from around 1235 until 1247, with the consecration of the chapel on completion of the works. As regards the artists working it is evident that the three cycles can be directly related to frescoes within the Roman domain of the first half of the 13th century, among them we recall those of the chapel of S. Gregorio al Sacro Speco at Subiaco (1228), the church of S. Nicola at Filettino and the crypt of the Duomo at Anagni (dating variously to the years 1227-1231 or to 1250 at the time of the bishop Pandolfo Conti (1237-1256); Pope Alexander IV reconsecrated the crypt in 1255). All the cited examples, in fact, appear to have some of their craftsmen in common, who vary according to the period of execution and to the importance also in size of the construction sites. In particular, both in the Anagni Crypt and at Ss. Quattro a numerous group of artists belonging to different workshops, of which two, namely those of the so-called *Maestro Ornatista* and *Terzo Maestro*, were present on both sites. Among the artists working in the Roman hall we also seem to be able to distinguish the hand of Giunta Pisano, whose presence in Rome in 1239 is suggested by a document signed by his son and servant at the nearby Basilica of San Clemente.

The frescoes of Ss. Quattro not only have the same cultural base but also the same ideological and political significance in common with the above-mentioned examples as regards the power struggle between the papacy and the emperor Frederick II. In particular, in the chapel of St Sylvester the message of the pope's supremacy over the emperor and of the legitimacy of his temporal sovereignty, themes typical of the Frederick II era, is elucidated by Constantine's attribution of the symbols of imperial power - the white horse, tiara and red cloak - to Sylvester. It is therefore no accident that on the east wall of the north bay the *Virtues* trample upon as many as three emperors: Nero, Alexander the Great and Julian the Apostate. And in relation to this, the call for a return to the magnificence of ancient Rome, pres-

ent in many iconographic motifs as well as in the decorative elements inspired by classical models, assumes not only an aesthetic value, but also a precise political significance: the popes are the new rulers of the eternal city, heirs of the ancient emperors. The cycles could be interpreted at different levels, but fully understood only by those who possessed the necessary preparation, and therefore by the members of the papal court. Of the latter, the frescoes also indicate the taste and, moreover, the international culture (many persons of rank, like Stefano Conti himself, had

Fig. 132. *Gothic hall. Personification of a* River *or of* Abundance.

Fig. 133. *Gothic hall. East wall of north bay.*

Fig. 134. *Gothic hall.* Amor celestis *with St Francis on her shoulder and Julian the Apostate at her feet and* Emulatio sancta *with St Dominic on her shoulder and Simon the Sorcerer and* Emulatio perversa *at her feet. To the left, the enlargement of the window and consequent partial destruction of the fresco is evident.*

studied outside Rome, in Paris, Bologna, and had travelled in Europe), which, on the one hand, fused the new Gothic contributions with their well-documented naturalism deriving principally from the illuminated manuscripts and, on the other, the call for a return to classical models with the Roman mediaeval tradition.

It must lastly be noted that not only the rooms mentioned, but the whole palace was covered with frescoes, of which few traces remain, sufficient however to suggest their importance: this was an ensemble of such wealth as to ensure that the *pulchrae picturae* (beautiful paintings) present in the complex would be explicitly mentioned at the end of the 14th century, and again in 1444-46, the humanist Biondo Flavio would describe it as *palatium insigne* (palace of great distinction).

Fig. 135. *Gothic hall.* The chariots of the Sun and Moon.

4.7. The exterior

Imposing structures overlook Via dei Ss. Quattro. As regards this road, it must be remembered that its plan is artificial in that it has been laid, at least partially, on Roman structures perhaps built to confine the slope of the hill. Descending from the corner of the façade, we encounter the flank of the quadriporticus of Leo IV, with large tufa blocks at its base. Following this, a construction in *tufelli* masonry dating to the 13th century backs onto the Great Tower: its more modest proportions typical of a simple residential dwelling suggest that it was a secondary residence, perhaps built for the chaplain (a function that in some way it still maintains, given that at least during the 18th century, the priest who officiated at the basilica lived there). About halfway down the slope, the Great Tower soars upwards, flanked by two imposing buttresses and pierced with numerous windows of varying shapes and sizes. At its summit a row of standard-bearing rings made of stone runs uninterrupted around the building. On the north side, the upper floor of the tower stands back to allow space for the external balcony to which access was gained directly from the hall. The imprint left by the parapet remains on the north-west buttress. As indicated by a corner section of the tower – chamfered to facilitate transit - the balcony continued for a short distance on the east side from where another door in the hall provided access to the balcony.

An imposing brick wall flanks the tower on the west side. The lower section is actually a cladding of tufa blocks that acted as a retaining wall for the residential quarters of the clergy at the time of Leo IV. In the upper section of the wall, filled-in openings of varying sizes testify to the complex history of the building. The final level, which has almost completely collapsed, corresponded to the hall with ogival windows (still visible in a drawing by the Dutch painter Bartholomew Breenbergh), which backed onto the tower making it necessary to modify its windows.

Descending still further a protruding tower stands out among another series of buildings, one on top of the other. An early 20th-century building then obliges the visitor to turn left at the corner into the modern Via dei Querceti to then

Fig. 136. *The structures of the Cardinal's palace seen from the surrounding rooftops.*

Fig. 137. *The Great Tower seen from Via dei Ss. Quattro: above, the filled-in doors and windows of the Gothic hall and traces of the external balcony can be noted.*

Fig. 138. *The great apse (photo: L. Barelli).*

catch sight of the structures of the chapel of St Nicholas, transformed into a tower in the 13th century, and those of the left aisle of the Leonine basilica, sustained at its corner by a massive brick buttress and elevated in the modern era to build a dormitory above. From Via dei Querceti, it is possible to admire the apse in all its glory, whose masonry surfaces reveal that they belong to different phases, underlined by the varying alignments of holes used to support the scaffolding during construction: the base, which lies on Roman ruins, up to the offset belongs to the 4th-century hall. Above, in the right half, the 4th-century masonry extends up to an area of bricks at the side of the central window, above which the 9th-century wall continues, recognizable by its crude workmanship. The whole left half belongs to the restoration works of Pascal II, to whom we also owe the remains of the cornice with marble corbels. The band of masonry above the latter and the roof, instead, derive from Cardinal Mellini's works in 1621.

To the right of the apse, we can then admire the *palatium dormidorii*, built in the first half of the 13th century to house the cells of the monks of Sassovivo. This rests directly on the apse, of which it blocks out a window, and terminates to the south with a diagonally positioned tower of the same period. This follows the orientation of the underlying Roman structures, whose remains were still visible at the base of the façade up until the 1940s, when shanty structures encroached upon the curtilage of the monument, one of many cases in the city where the absence of controls resulted in illegal building.

The splendid façade of the *palatium* presents a curtain-wall of recovered Roman bricks of excellent manufacture and was pierced by two rows of rectangular windows, today filled in, with marble frames surmounted by a system of small relieving arches, the largest of which is pointed, alternating with two orders of oculi, coinciding with the small splayed interior windows. Two bands of plaster, at the height of the window sills and architrave respectively, run along the entire façade and round the corner tower; the plaster, incised and painted to resemble bricks, also covered the arched lintels of the openings. Two doors on the first floor overlooked a wooden balcony, of which the thick holes from the supporting beams are easily visible. Lastly, the remains of a latrine chute can be noted on the right side of the tower.

Fig. 139. *The west wall of the Benedictine monastery (photo: L. Barelli).*

Selected bibliography

The principal historical texts that deal specifically with the monumental complex are as follows:

Apollonj Ghetti B.M., *I Ss. Quattro Coronati*, Rome 1964 (Le chiese di Roma illustrate, 81).

Barberini M. G., *I Santi Quattro Coronati a Roma*, Rome 1989 (Itinerari d'arte e cultura – Basiliche).

de Rossi G.B., *I Santi Quattro Coronati e la loro chiesa sul Celio*, in «Bullettino di Archeologia Cristiana», 1879, pp. 45-90.

Krautheimer R., Corbett S., *I Ss. Quattro Coronati*, in Krautheimer R., Corbett S., Frankl W., *Corpus Basilicarum Christianarum Romae*, IV, Vatican City, 1976, pp. 1-34.

Manzi P., *Il convento fortificato dei Ss. Quattro Coronati nella storia e nell'arte*, in «Bollettino dell'Istituto Storico e di Cultura dell'Arma del Genio», part I, 32, 1966, pp. 505-545; part II, 33, 1967, pp. 8-63; 223-258.

Memmolo D., *Della vita, chiesa et reliquie de' Santi Quattro Coronati*, Rome 1628.

Muñoz A., *Il restauro della chiesa e del chiostro dei Ss. Quattro Coronati*, Rome 1914.

Ugonio P., *Historia delle stationi di Roma, che si celebrano la quadragesima, dove... si tratta delle origini, fondationi, siti, restauratione, ornamenti, reliquie et memorie di esse chiese...*, Rome 1588.

For a more comprehensive and up-to-date bibliography:

Barelli L., *Il palazzo cardinalizio dei Ss. Quattro Coronati a Roma nel basso medioevo*, in *Il Lazio tra antichità e medioevo. Studi in memoria di Jean Coste*, edited by Z. Mari, M.T. Petrara, M. Sperandio, Rome 1999, pp. 111-124.

Barelli L., Ecclesiam reparare*: Pasquale II (1099-1118) e il restauro della basilica dei Ss. Quattro Coronati a Roma*, in «Palladio», N.S., XIX, n. 38 July-December 2006, pp. 5-29.

Barelli L., *L'esperienza interdisciplinare del restauro del chiostro dei Ss. Quattro Coronati in Roma*, in *Trattato di restauro architettonico. Terzo aggiornamento. Grandi temi di restauro*, diretto da Giovanni Carbonara, Utet, Turin 2008, pp. 1-24.

Barelli L., Pugliese R., Sadori L., *Nuovi dati dallo scavo del chiostro del complesso dei Ss. Quattro Coronati a Roma*, in «Rendiconti della Pontificia Accademia Romana di Archeologia», 80 (2007-2008), pp. 77-121.

Draghi A., *Gli affreschi dell'Aula gotica nel Monastero dei Santi Quattro Coronati. Una storia ritrovata*, Milan 2006.

La fontana del chiostro. Storia e restauri, a cura di Lia Barelli, Rome 2006.

Filippi Moretti G., *I SS. Quattro Coronati. Nuove acquisizioni dai restauri architettonici*, in «Monumenti di Roma», III, nos. 1/2, January/December 2004, pp. 114-120.

Guiglia Guidobaldi A., *Il reimpiego delle mensole altomedievali nel XII secolo. I casi dei SS. Quattro Coronati e di S. Clemente a Roma*, in *Il reimpiego in architettura. Recupero, trasformazione, uso*, edited by Jean-François Bernard, Philippe Bernardi e Daniela Esposito, Conference Proceedings 8-10 November 2007, École Française de Rome 2008 (Collection de l'École Française de Rome, 418), pp. 109-121.

Monache Agostiniane del Monastero dei Santi Quattro Coronati
Via dei Santi Quattro, 20 - 00184 Roma - Tel. 06 70475427
email: monacheosasantiquattro@tin.it

Finito di stampare nel mese di dicembre 2009 presso la CDC Arti Grafiche, Città di Castello (Perugia)